To:

_____

From:

_____

Date:

_____

Mini Devotions: Grace for Today
Published by Christian Art Publishers
PO Box 1599, Vereeniging, 1930, RSA

© 2019
First edition 2019

Devotions compiled from *One-Minute Devotions® Grace for Today*
by Solly Ozrovech

Cover designed by Christian Art Publishers

Designed by Christian Art Publishers

Images used under license from Shutterstock.com

Printed in China

ISBN 978-1-4321-3141-8

23 24 25 26 27 28 29 30 31 32 – 26 25 24 23 22 21 20 19 18

MINI DEVOTIONS

Grace
FOR
TODAY

CHRISTIAN ART
PUBLISHERS

The Grace of a New Beginning

He who was seated on the throne said,
"I am making everything new!"

Revelation 21:5

It is a sign of God's immeasurable grace that no person ever reaches a stage in life where one cannot start over. Each day that dawns is a new beginning. Our God is the God of second chances.

Do not allow whatever may have happened in the past to cause you to lose sight of what the future may hold. If you wish to make a fresh start, make a firm decision to be done with your old life, even though it will still try to enslave you.

All new life comes from God alone. Continually affirm that new life flows through you as a result of God's grace, and you will receive the inheritance of new life that is yours in Christ.

Lord of new beginnings, thank You that each new day
Your mercies are new and I can begin again. Amen.

Eternal Life

For this very reason, Christ died and
returned to life so that He might be the
Lord of both the dead and the living.

Romans 14:9

Many people brood over the unknown. In their uncertainty they fall prey to anxiety and tension.

For the Christian believer there is a glorious truth that emanates from the life, death, and resurrection of Jesus Christ. We know that He is with us right now, leading us through life. He also went to prepare a place for us in God's heavenly kingdom. In this way He assures us that when our earthly life is over, we will be with the Lord forever.

Instead of being consumed with fear and worry, hold on to the promises of Jesus and rejoice in the fact that because Jesus lives, you too will live forever.

Risen Savior, through faith I know that You live
and that I too will live eternally with You. Amen.

God Works in Everyday Things

In his heart a man plans his course,
but the LORD determines his steps.

Proverbs 16:9

God often works in miraculous ways. We see His glory in the changing heavens; we see His handiwork in the grandeur of Creation.

Yet, God is also the Creator of the small and everyday things: the perfection of the rose and the fragility of the forget-me-not. All of these things reflect a creative God who is also the Master of order and detail.

We so easily forget that God is interested in our well-being. Just consider how many times He has guided you through difficult circumstances.

Thank You, Almighty God, that You never cease
to work in my life and answer my prayers.
You speak with a thousand tongues;
let me always hear Your voice. Amen.

A Child of the King

You are all sons of God through faith in Christ
Jesus, for all of you who were baptized into
Christ have clothed yourselves with Christ.

Galatians 3:26-27

You never need to feel spiritually inferior – especially in comparison to other believers. Remember that when God accepted you as His child, He did not do so on the basis of your knowledge, work or worthiness. In His grace He accepted you based entirely on your faith in Jesus Christ and your acceptance of Him as your Redeemer and Savior.

Jesus accepts you for who and what you are. All He asks is that you believe in Him and accept Him as the Lord of your life. Joyfully respond to this invitation and experience the grace and love of your divine Father every day.

Holy God, my heavenly Father, thank
You that I can, through faith, claim the
privilege of being called Your child. Amen.

The Grace of God

Grace and peace be yours in abundance.

1 Peter 1:2

People are always searching for peace to help them deal with their problems. Do not be tempted to seek man-made solutions, as there is only one true method of handling your life with confidence and assurance – and that is in the power of Jesus Christ.

If you commit yourself and your life to Him unconditionally, then you can rest assured that He will give you the grace required to handle every problem. You will thus be blessed with tranquility and peace far beyond human understanding.

Grace and peace become a reality in your life only through God, so don't drift from Him and forfeit what only He can give.

Loving Master, I thank You, because through
Your grace You enable me to face and handle
every problem that comes my way. Amen.

Indescribable Grace

"My grace is sufficient for you, for My
power is made perfect in weakness."

2 Corinthians 12:9

When you find yourself in a situation that makes you feel incompetent and inadequate, do not focus on your own abilities. Jesus made it very clear that we are capable of doing nothing without Him, but with Him we can do anything.

In this truth lies the answer to all your fears, doubts and insecurities. Whatever you do in life, first take it to God in prayer, seek His help and lay all your expectations, fears and concerns before Him.

By allowing Him to work through you, you will achieve the kind of success that would otherwise be unattainable in your own strength.

Loving Father, I praise You and thank You for the
wonderful assurance that I can do all things
through Christ who gives me strength. Amen.

God's Grace Is Sufficient

The days of the blameless are known to the LORD,
and their inheritance will endure forever.

Psalm 37:18

We often hear of people who apparently live virtuous lives and yet are plagued by disaster. Sometimes we want to question God's actions, and it is difficult to agree with Paul when he says, "We know that in all things God works for the good of those who love Him, who have been called according to His purpose" (Rom. 8:28).

However, it is important to remember that God's perspective on life is eternal and He truly desires all things to work for your own good. Paul also says that our present suffering does not outweigh the glory that will be revealed in us (see Rom. 8:18). Take courage and let your heart be peaceful – God's grace is sufficient!

I thank You, all-knowing God, that Your grace is always sufficient for me, despite my problems. Amen.

Focus on God

In all your ways acknowledge Him, and
He will make your paths straight.

Proverbs 3:6

Life can suddenly become filled with problems of all kinds. Regardless of their source, they dominate your life until you find a solution.

If you are experiencing a problem and sincerely seek a solution, direct your thoughts to God and don't focus on the problem. You won't find a solution if you do not allow God to assist you.

Allow Him to create order from chaos and to give you the right solution. When God becomes more important than your problem, you will be fueled by a spiritual power because God is occupying His rightful place in your life. You will find solutions to your problems and by His grace live victoriously.

Eternal God, I put You first in my life, knowing that You are powerful enough to handle every crisis in my life. Amen.

God Makes Life Good

"Listen to this, Job; stop and consider God's wonders."

Job 37:14

We live in troubled times where it is easy to give up and succumb to worldly temptations.

Instead, pause, and reflect on the grace and wonderful deeds of God. Out of the chaos and darkness He created this beautiful earth. He loved us so much that He saved us from the bonds of sin and death.

Through the life of Jesus Christ, He gave us an example of the fullness of life.

He promises us eternal and abundant life. Praise Him for all His wonderful deeds, and for His wonderful gift of grace.

Lord, how You fill my heart with gladness. Thank You for Your glorious deeds that I see all around me. Amen.

Grace and Peace in God

I lay down and slept, yet I woke up in safety,
for the LORD was watching over me.

Psalm 3:5 NLT

History shows us that those people who walked intimately with God found hidden resources of strength to overcome their setbacks. Those who have an unflinching faith in the living Christ will not waver or break under attacks. Those who put their trust in the all-encompassing love of Christ will not give in to the icy touch of fear.

The same Christ who hushed the wind and stilled the storm at sea when the disciples were panic-stricken, is calling out to you today, "Be strong and courageous; do not be afraid!" Put your trust in Him and experience how His love and grace cause the storms in your life to subside.

O Lord, I'm so insecure about the future, so
uncertain about what lies ahead. Help me
to put my trust in You day by day. Amen.

Glory in His Grace

The grace of the Lord Jesus be with God's people. Amen.

Revelation 22:21

The last words of the Bible are this wonderful benediction. How these words soothe our storm-tossed hearts!

We all, at one time or another, find ourselves suffering from anxiety – either because of a current situation or because we fear the future. In our human weakness and short-sightedness we are not sure how to act. Some people try to handle everything in their own strength, while others throw their hands up in despair.

Remember, the only way out of a problem, and the only reason for success, is the compassionate love and grace of our heavenly Father. The saving and sustaining grace of God permeates our lives. Because He loves you, He blesses you with His grace.

O Lord, I thank You for Your grace.

You saved me and redeemed me from death.

You are my heart's desire. Amen.

Grace – Rich and Free!

The grace of our Lord Jesus Christ be with you all.

2 Thessalonians 3:18

Where would we be if it were not for the grace of God? The wonderful song *Amazing Grace* tells of a prodigal son who came back to the Father's house.

John Newton, the writer of the song, says that he was spiritually blind and lost, but the grace of God touched and healed him. This song reminds us of a redeeming God whose love is so great that He gave us His all through grace.

The Son of God took your guilt and my guilt upon Himself and sacrificed His life to redeem us from sin. His grace extends so far that even when we turn away from Him, Christ waits patiently and lovingly for us to turn back to Him.

Thank You, God, that Your grace has set me free
and given me new hope for tomorrow. Amen.

Sufficient Grace

"You then, my son, be strong in
the grace that is in Christ Jesus."

2 Timothy 2:1

Many people are not able to work through the problems they face and fear has a devastating effect on them.

Jesus invites those who are tired and heavy-laden to bring their problems to Him and find rest for their souls. He invites you to bring your anxieties to Him because He cares for you. Turn to God, He will enable you to handle your problems with courage.

Receive your strength and confidence from Him because in all circumstances His grace will be more than sufficient for you so that you can deal with your problems in a new, assured manner.

Father, I ask for Your strength to assist me
in times of weakness, help me to know
Your grace that is sufficient for me. Amen.

Together with God

I can do everything through
Him who gives me strength.

Philippians 4:13

When you think of God in all His glory and of yourself as an insignificant speck on the earth, it is incredibly difficult to identify with Him.

And yet, the Spirit of God who fills God's entire creation, can also inhabit your spirit. When you realize this, you release a previously untapped power in your life.

When you realize that God, in His grace, has revealed Himself in you through His Spirit, you will learn to draw on His strength, and your life will be vibrant and balanced.

Merciful Lord Jesus, I accept the gift of the Holy
Spirit and therefore enjoy intimate communion
with You, my Lord and my God. Amen.

When Things Go Wrong

"To whom do you belong, and where are you going,
and who owns all these animals in front of you?"

Genesis 32:17

Life must have purpose and significance if you are
to live meaningfully. One of the great truths of
the Christian life is that it changes your attitude.
Previously you lived without hope or expectation,
but Christ now plants new hope in your heart. When
you truly start living in Christ, you begin to look at
life with new understanding.

You will never again have to ask, "Is life worth-
while?" When the thoughts of Christ fill you and
the Holy Spirit's strength saturates your spirit, you
realize the rich quality of your faith, and your life
takes on new and exciting dimensions.

Lord Jesus, You came so that we may have life in
abundance. Help me to remember to come to You
when days are dark, so that my life may be infused
with significance and meaning once again. Amen.

The Coming Grace

Concerning this salvation, the prophets,
who spoke of the grace that was to come to you,
searched intently and with the greatest care.

1 Peter 1:10

As believers we sometimes sense that God allows certain things to happen; that He has planned wonderful circumstances and has stretched out His holy hand to make sure that everything works out well for all of us.

The grace of God pours out of the loving heart of God and changes people's lives wherever it goes. It is also destined for you. It will transform you, empower you, build you up spiritually and give you a purpose in life. It will not remove all hardships from your life, but it will give you more resources to help you cope. It is destined for you. Have you received it?

We praise and thank You, Lord Jesus, for those who have
received Your grace and shared it with others. Amen.

Praise Be to the Lord

Praise be to the LORD, for He has heard my cry for mercy. The LORD is my strength and my shield; my heart trusts in Him, and I am helped. My heart leaps for joy and I will give thanks to Him in song.

Psalm 28:6-7

When we pray for God's grace we should never forget to sing His praises as well. He is our only hope, our strength and our shield. Even while we are waiting for Him to deliver us from our present dilemmas, we can praise Him for His faithfulness in the past. Then our faith in the mercy of God will be strengthened.

God is merciful! How often have we been on the verge of giving up in despair because our situation seemed completely hopeless, and then God stepped in and acted on our behalf?

The might of God works in our favor when we call on Him in faith, and then we can give thanks to Him in song.

I praise You, Lord, because You
heard my cry for mercy. Amen.

Our Hope Is in You

Do any of the worthless idols of the nations bring
rain? Do the skies themselves send down showers?
No, it is You, O LORD our God. Therefore our hope
is in You, for You are the one who does all this.

Jeremiah 14:22

God is our only hope in every situation. When we feel
utterly helpless, depend on God and He will bring you
through every trial. If God is our only hope then we
need to be prepared and have enough faith to wait
for the Lord to take action.

If you are suffering as a result of sin, like the people
of Judah in today's Scripture verse, then confess it.
Sin brings only pain and suffering, but God brings
redemption. Confess your sin to Him and take comfort in the incredible, undeserved grace that God
offers to each of His children.

Holy God, I confess my sins with deep remorse
and know that You will not cast me away,
but will embrace me with forgiveness. Amen.

God's Faithful Love

You forgave the iniquity of Your people and covered
all their sins. You set aside all Your wrath and
turned from Your fierce anger. Will you not revive
us again, that Your people may rejoice in You?

Psalm 85:2-3, 6

It has become common nowadays to deny sin and
its consequences, but there are millions of people
who live under the burden of their sin.

A feeling of guilt is often a gift of God's grace to
give our lives new meaning, to lead us to a new and
more productive life. But an even greater gift from
God is His grace that allows us to move in a new
direction once our sins have been forgiven.

If we just confess our sin and ask for forgiveness
then God is merciful and will forgive us. Think of all
that He has already forgiven and give Him praise.

I thank and praise You, Lord, my God, that in
Your mercy You have forgiven all my sins and
helped me to bear fruit to Your glory. Amen.

God's Great Gift

May the grace of the Lord Jesus Christ,
and the love of God, and the fellowship
of the Holy Spirit be with you all.

2 Corinthians 13:14

In these materialistic days, it is a real problem for many people to appreciate a precious gift that cannot be valued in monetary terms.

Nevertheless, when you reflect on the sacrifice that God made at Golgotha, the redemption, salvation and hope that He gave us, it should be a source of inspiration and wonder.

There is no way in which we, as humans, could justly repay the Lord for His unfathomable love. Yet, we can open our lives to Him so that through the love of God and the grace of Jesus Christ, the Holy Spirit will enable us to do His work and to spread His love amongst all we come into contact with.

Lord, I always want to glorify You as my Father.
Guide me through Your Holy Spirit so that I may
be obedient to You in everything I do. Amen.

God's Grace-Filled Love

May the Lord direct your hearts into
God's love and Christ's perseverance.

2 Thessalonians 3:5

We cherish in our hearts the eternal truth that God's love is free and undeserved. Nothing that you have done or intend to do can earn you that.

God loves you because God is love, and this is a great truth for which we are eternally grateful and for which we should glorify and thank Him.

You are the object of God's love. God Himself lit the flame of love for Him in your heart, so you must do all you can to ensure that nothing extinguishes this inner flame inside you.

Truly, You are love! Your Son became
man to demonstrate true love, Father.
Help me to radiate love in return. Amen.

The Man of Sorrows

He was despised and rejected by men, a
Man of sorrows, and familiar with suffering.

Isaiah 53:3

Christ's suffering was unique and stands out in world history. It emerges from the plains of time as a monument of remembrance to the Man of sorrows' suffering – for you and me. It reminds us that God's grace does not come cheap: the price was suffering, sorrow and blood; the blood of His only Son who became human for our sake.

Jesus, the One without sin, in obedience to the Father, became sin for our sakes. The unbearable burden of the sins of all people through the ages was placed on His shoulders and He vicariously carried it to Golgotha.

Lord Jesus, it was for me that You had to endure
scorn and suffering, for me that You had to be
crucified. Thank You, Jesus, that You died for
me so that I may inherit everlasting life. Amen.

Seek to Please God

For they loved praise from men
more than praise from God.

John 12:43

The only way to achieve the very best in life, and to develop the feeling of self-confidence and fulfillment that is so essential to your peace of mind, is to stay true in all things to your high calling in Jesus.

He is constant – yesterday, today and for all eternity. He will never forsake you or fail you.

Place your full trust in Him and not in fallible people. You will never be disappointed.

We do not understand it, Lord, but Your way
is always best. You will never forsake us and
we know that we are safe in You. Amen.

He Helps Us to Succeed

By the grace of God I am what I am, and
His grace to me was not without effect.

1 Corinthians 15:10

There are many people who declare that they are "self-made people" and that their success is solely through their own doing.

It is a foolish person indeed who convinces himself that the honor for his accomplishments is his alone. Everyone faces problems and stumbling blocks in their careers. If God's hand of grace was not shielding you, you would never have triumphed over your problems and adversities.

By gratefully acknowledging the Father in your achievements, and by thanking Him for His grace and goodness, an extra dimension of joy and happiness will be added to your life.

Thank You for blessing us so undeservedly and
so abundantly, Lord. You are our salvation
and courage for each day. Amen.

When God Lives in You

If anyone acknowledges that Jesus is the
Son of God, God lives in him and he in God.

1 John 4:15

The simple teachings of Jesus Christ have enormous power and if you embrace God, you will have a force in your life like you have never experienced before.

The miraculous truth is that you will not live alone with God, but He will live in you. This is the most amazing and significant experience that you will ever witness; your disposition towards people and circumstances changes; you notice the beauty of life instead of focusing on its dreariness; your objectives are creative and you work positively toward them.

Acknowledging Christ results in such far-reaching consequences that you will stand in wonder each day at what God has achieved in your life through His grace.

I wish to celebrate Your strength. Make me
victorious in battle through Your Spirit. Amen.

Inconceivable Grace

"So is My word that goes out from My
mouth: It will not return to Me empty,
but will accomplish what I desire and
achieve the purpose for which I sent it."

Isaiah 55:11

Lord, my God, I glorify and praise Your holy name.
Your love knows no boundaries! I meditate on Your
promises; may Your precious words become part of
my thoughts, life and conduct.

Stand by me through the Holy Spirit so that I will
always have a warm heart for others, so that I may
perform the true service of love, in Your name and
to Your glory.

Let me never forget how dependent I am on
You. I will always hold firmly onto Your hand and so
inherit Your kingdom.

Lord, soften my heart to others so I may glorify
Your name. I ask for all this through the blood
of Jesus, my Savior and Redeemer. Amen.

Now and Then

Now we see but a poor reflection as in
a mirror; then we shall see face to face.

1 Corinthians 13:12

"Now" and "then" are two little words with profound meaning. While we are in this life "now" we have to contend with many situations that look very dark and problematic.

But how blessed and happy we will be when we remember both sides of His promise: "now" is a mirror and a poor reflection, but "then" we will see all the glory that God has prepared for His children.

One day we will come face-to-face with our Lord, and only then will we discover how often His love and grace shielded us from disaster and danger.

I thank You, my Lord, that Your love and grace
guide me from day to day. With this blessed
assurance I praise and glorify You all my life. Amen.

Provider of Needs

God is able to make all grace abound to you, so that in all things at all times, having all that you need, you will abound in every good work.

2 Corinthians 9:8

God loves the generous giver and blesses him. God Himself gives abundantly so that His children may have enough in all things. He gave His Son, the Holy Spirit, and the excitement of a new, redeemed life. God promises us that we will have all that we need.

If we trust in the Lord completely, we can be certain, regardless of how dark the storm clouds are above us, how great the need – we will always have sufficient strength and grace we only need to ask God to provide in our need.

From His unfathomable grace, He will every day, in every way, provide in all our needs through life. His love knows no bounds!

Thank You for the quiet assurance, Lord Jesus, that I will always have sufficient strength and grace for every situation in life. Amen.

God Loves You Dearly

"I have loved you," says the LORD.
"But you ask, 'How have You loved us?'"

Malachi 1:2

People who have been hurt or broken by life tend to have a problem acknowledging that God is a God of love. You must remember that the love of God is boundless and infinite.

It is an unconditional, limitless, eternal love in comparison to our love that is of a passing nature. God's love and care for us is based on that which is good for us, not only now, but in the future as well.

The extent of God's love is so infinite that He is by your side in every situation of life. He waits to support and help you; console you; to help you overcome stumbling blocks, and to be your Shepherd.

Thank You, God of love, that I will sit down
one day at the feast of the Lamb, because
I love You and You love me. Amen.

The Feast of God's Grace

The angel said to her, "Do not be afraid,
Mary, you have found favor with God."

Luke 1:30

God is no respecter of persons – all people are equal before Him. God has no favorites, but He is selective.

Through the responsibility placed on her, Mary revealed the quality of her life and her devotion to the heavenly Father. As far as it is known, she led a quiet life somewhere in the hills of Judea, unknown except to her family. And yet she was chosen above all women as God's instrument through which He would reveal Himself to the world.

Your love for and devotion to God may seem unimportant, but if you offer Him your very best, He will use you in His own unique way. Then you will experience the feast of God's grace.

I praise and thank You, Father, that You reveal Yourself
time and again to me. Use me as an instrument
to spread Your love through the world. Amen.

Our Shepherd

The LORD is my shepherd, I shall not be in want.

Psalm 23:1

Those of us who belong to the Lord know we are safe and secure. We know for certain that the Lord is our Shepherd. Therefore we do not fear the future because He is already there. He will walk before us every day, leading us to our eternal destination.

Sometimes we have doubts about the future. We wonder whether we will have enough to provide for our essential needs. With childlike certainty, the psalmist then tells us, "I shall not be in want." You shall not be "in want" of anything that you truly need and that is good for you. The Lord will hear when you call, because His love never changes.

Lord God, it is a glorious reassurance to me
that You are my Shepherd and that in
Your hands I am safe and secure. Amen.

Spiritual Maturity

You, however, are controlled not by the sinful nature
but by the Spirit, if the Spirit of God lives in you.

Romans 8:9

The direction that your life has taken reveals where
the emphasis in your life lies. You may achieve your
material objectives, but is that enough? Is that why
God gave you life?

Remember, you are also a spiritual being, therefore, your spirit can only ever be fully satisfied when
it is in a dynamic relationship with the Holy Spirit.

This intimately personal relationship with God
can only be attained by faith in the resurrected
Christ; a faith that is more than a fleeting emotion; a
faith that accepts His authority in all aspects of life.
This type of faith will give true sense and meaning
to your life.

I never want to be separated from You, Lord. I wish
to experience Your love and be a fruitful vine
in Your kingdom. I want to glorify You. Amen.

Storm Clouds Gather

Surely God is my salvation; I will trust and not
be afraid. The LORD, the LORD, is my strength
and my song; He has become my salvation.

Isaiah 12:2

It is a fact of life that sometimes storm clouds gather,
darkening our lives, and it is futile to ignore them,
hoping they will disappear. Instead, stand firm with
a living faith in the Almighty God, who controls the
storms of life.

However threatening the circumstances of life
may be, it is imperative that you do not allow anything to take God's central role in your life. With
Him as the center you will maintain your balance.
The ominous clouds might still be present, but you
will be assured that your loving Father is working
everything together for your good.

Even when everything around me is shrouded in
darkness, You will shield me. Thank You, Father. Amen.

Get the Most from Your Faith

"Whoever has will be given more, whoever does not have, even what he has will be taken from him."

Matthew 13:12

Unfortunately, some people have never been inspired to walk intimately with the Lord. As a result of this, their faith is weak and their discipleship is ineffectual.

The world needs disciplined Christians to affirm and proclaim the teachings of Jesus, particularly His command, "As I have loved you, so you must love one another" (John 13:34).

The discipline that is needed to live a life of Christian love demands a strength that can only come from the Holy Spirit. This is nurtured through prayer, Bible study and a hunger for a more profound experience with God.

I plead with You, O Jesus, for the gift of Your Holy Spirit so that my faith can be fully experienced. Amen.

Faith Is a Process of Growth

Grow in the grace and knowledge of
our Lord and Savior Jesus Christ.

2 Peter 3:18

It is sad to note that many Christians make little progress in their spiritual lives after accepting Christ as their Savior.

Ask yourself: Is Christ becoming more real to me? Is prayer essential in my decision-making? Do I find God's will for my life in the Scriptures? Am I nearer to Christ than I was when I was born again?

It takes courage to answer these questions. Allow this to be a prelude to renewing your faith in Christ and there will be no end to the growth and development it will bring forth. This growth will bring life-giving energy, enabling you to develop in Christlikeness and bear fruit in God's kingdom.

You are the true Vine, Lord. Keep me from evil
and help me to be truly fruitful in You. Amen.

An Enriching Experience

"Remain in Me, and I will remain in you."

John 15:4

It is worth remembering that the stars are still shining, even when clouds hide them. Remember, too, that behind the dark patches of life, the eternal love of your heavenly Father is still shining brightly. If you have cultivated trust in Him, your faith will carry you through the darkest moments of life.

The life that Jesus promises us if we remain in Him is such a challenge that people hesitate to accept it and instead choose to remain in a religious rut that promotes neither joy nor spiritual growth.

The life that Christ promises is much more than just an emotional experience. It creates inner peace, a constructive purpose in life, and provides the strength to achieve and maintain such a life through the power of the Holy Spirit.

Holy Father, I praise and glorify You for the life-changing strength that flows from Christ. Amen.

God Is in Control

Job replied to the LORD: "I know that You can do
all things; no plan of Yours can be thwarted."

Job 42:1

No matter where you go you will meet pessimistic
people – people who see no hope for the future and
carry an atmosphere of gloom around with them.

Rather than give in to despair, consider the
greatness of God. Look back over the years and you
will find many examples of the wonderful ways in
which God transforms despair into hope; sorrow
into joy; and defeat into victory.

When things around you appear dark and terri-
fying, hold on to the promises of God. Remember the
mighty deeds that He has performed, and continue in
confidence and with the certain knowledge that He is
wholly in control.

Almighty God and loving Father, my heart's
knowledge that You are in control allows me
to be courageous even in dark days. Guide me
on Your path and keep my faith strong. Amen.

Just Believe

"Don't be afraid; just believe."

Mark 5:36

Many Christians urge fellow believers to, "Just believe!" but it's not always as easy as that, especially when the storm clouds close in around you.

Fortunately, through the grace of God it is easy to develop a mature and sincere faith. Recall an incident in your life when something out of the ordinary happened and thank God for it. It might not be something big or significant, but when you recall the incident, it strengthens your faith in a wonderful way.

Make a habit of remembering small answers to prayer, and your faith will gradually grow to the extent where you will receive bigger revelations from God.

Loving Master, I want to grow in my faith
so that I can bring glory and honor to
You in everything I do and say. Amen.

Believing without Seeing

Therefore we are always confident.
We live by faith, not by sight.

2 Corinthians 5:6-7

When you are facing problems, difficulties or tough decisions, do you trust God sufficiently to put yourself and your future in His hands?

Jesus came to confirm that God loves you unconditionally. His care, help and compassion are unquestionable. You are precious in God's sight. Therefore, Christ will not allow anything to harm you. He will always be with you.

With this assurance, you can trust God unconditionally in everything. Then you will walk along His path, doing His will.

If you do this, you will experience peace and tranquility of mind. Even if you cannot see the complete road ahead, faith will carry you through.

Lord, please be with me in the dark days, and
shine the light of Your presence before
me so that I do not stumble. Amen.

Trust in God

As for me, I watch in hope for the LORD, I wait
for God my Savior; my God will hear me.

Micah 7:7

Some people look at the stars or consult fortune-tellers in order to "see" their future.

However trustworthy these methods seem, they cannot help us handle the unknown. The only way in which we can be filled with confidence about the future is by believing in God.

When you are facing a problem and doubt tries to take hold of you, Jesus comes to you, saying, "Take courage! It is I. Don't be afraid" (Matt. 14:27). Christ Himself will bring you peace of mind.

Loving Savior, I place myself completely under
Your control, for I know that You alone
can guarantee me peace of mind. Amen.

Do You Truly Believe?

"I do believe; help me overcome my unbelief!"

Mark 9:24

How solid is your faith? Have you reduced it to outward matters of attending church, singing songs of praise, listening to nice sermons and trying to live a respectable life?

Your faith only becomes reality when the external ceremonies of Christianity become a pulsating and powerful experience in your soul. It becomes a reality when you no longer see yourself as someone defeated by sin because God's Holy Spirit, who resides in you, enables you to triumph over sin.

You must develop the discipline of experiencing Christ's presence in your everyday life. Prayer, Bible study and fellowship with other believers are essential to attaining a positive, living and dynamic faith.

Lord, You are my only shelter. When I feel powerless and afraid, You will lead me through the darkness and give me renewed courage. Amen.

The Light on Your Way

God said, "Let there be light," and there was light.

Genesis 1:3

When we look back along the road we have traveled, we tend to focus only on the negative things. Because the past had its share of problems, many people expect the same from the future.

But this is a negative way of looking at life. The prayer of your heart every day should be, "Lead me, O Light of the world!" Jesus Christ is still the Light of the world and He has promised that those who follow Him will never walk in darkness.

Take His hand in faith, and trust and experience Him as the light of your life.

> God of light and truth, thank You that Your
> Son has illuminated my life so that I can walk
> into the future in faith and trust. Be my light,
> even when darkness falls around me. Amen.

God Remains in Control

He is before all things, and in
Him all things hold together.

Colossians 1:17

There are times when it seems as if everything is going wrong. Throughout history, nations and individuals have struggled through disasters, hardships, dangers, sorrow and adversity.

Before you become despondent, however, acknowledge the greatness, glory and constancy of God. He called the world into existence, He created man and has kept vigil over His creation, caring for us through the ages and sheltering us in every disastrous storm.

He is the Creator God who will never abandon His workmanship. Hold onto His promises; place your entire trust in the living Christ and through Him you will survive all adversities.

You are eternal, Lord, and the workmanship of Your
Creation bears testimony to Your great glory. Amen.

Blessed Assurance

Commit to the LORD whatever you
do, and your plans will succeed.

Proverbs 16:3

Planning is important in every area of life. You plan for the future, for your marriage, for your finances and for retirement. Much of our time and energy goes into planning.

There is a way to make planning better, however, but it requires strict spiritual discipline to make it effective and it must be undertaken with sincerity and honesty. It also requires solid faith and trust in God and in His promises.

Whatever your concern may be, lay it before God in prayer with all your fears and expectations, trusting Him completely.

Leave the matter in God's hands. In His own perfect time and way, He will show you how to bring it to pass.

*Dear Lord, guide me to follow Your commands
and to fulfill Your will in obedience. Amen.*

Faith That Counts

The only thing that counts is faith
expressing itself through love.

Galatians 5:6

People have different opinions regarding what is most important in our spiritual lives.

Your faith will be insufficient and ineffective if it does not lead you to a more profound knowledge and awareness of God.

Faith is alive and meaningful when it is expressed through love. Without love, faith becomes dead and the height, depth and eternal nature of God's love cannot be experienced. If you possess a living faith, manifested in love, you have the basic qualities of a practical, inspired and effective religion that is acceptable to God.

Lord, Your Word teaches me to love You with
my whole heart, soul and mind, and to love
my neighbor as myself. Grant me the strength
to abide by these commandments. Amen.

God Has a Plan for You

Do not be distressed and do not be angry with
yourselves for selling me here, because it was
to save lives that God sent me ahead of you.

Genesis 45:5

It is often difficult to understand that God is fulfilling
His plan in your life, especially when times are tough.
When Joseph was sold into slavery, he probably
struggled to discern God's will. Nevertheless, many
years later, he recognized that God had been with him
through it all.

God determines the pattern of your life. In your
present circumstances, difficult as they might be, hold
on to the assurance that God is busy working out His
perfect plan for your life. Life's darkest moments can
become a testimony of God's perfect purpose for
your life.

Faithful Guide, I will trust You to lead me surely
along the pathways through life, even when
the dark shadows hide my way. Amen.

Conquer Depression

"For you who revere My name, the sun of
righteousness will rise with healing in its wings."

Malachi 4:2

Depression and pessimism are ailments that can
destroy a person's soul. Apart from the fact that
depression is an illness of the mind, it also affects your
physical and spiritual well-being, limits your vision of
the future, and negatively influences your attitude
towards life.

The only way to fight such an emotional disruption effectively is to turn to Christ and open yourself
to His love and healing.

Place yourself unconditionally in His care. When
Jesus guides you along the path you need to take
through life, you will be filled with a sense of self-
confidence and well-being that only He can give you.

I cling to You, Lord Jesus, in the knowledge
that nothing in this life can harm me
as long as You are with me. Amen.

Comfort in the Word

Open my eyes that I may see
wonderful things in Your law.

Psalm 119:18

Disillusionment and dejection are common among people who have developed a negative and pessimistic outlook on life.

In order to live and not merely exist, it is essential to nurture a positive attitude – even when things are not going well. Your faith will need to be strong if you are to triumph over your problems with joy.

Scripture is filled with stories of how ordinary people, like you and me, overcame hostile forces in the name of the Lord. Draw comfort from the Word and through Jesus Christ, the incarnate Word. Then you will be able to triumph over any adversity.

You reveal Yourself in Your Word. It is trustworthy,
steadfast and unfailing. Thank You that I can know
the abundant life that is found in Your Word. Amen.

His Eternal Love

Though I walk in the midst of trouble, You preserve
my life. The Lord will fulfill His purpose for me;
Your love, O Lord, endures forever – do
not abandon the works of Your hands.

Psalm 138:7-8

You might sometimes feel that God has abandoned
you when you needed Him most. But through faith
you need to hold fast to what you know is true about
God, even when you cannot see any results.

Although we are inclined to plan our whole course
through life, we can confess, together with David,
"The Lord will fulfill His purpose for me." In the time
of his worst trial, David still trusted God to protect
him. Be assured that the Lord will never neglect the
work of His hands, so even in the dark times, remember that God is faithful and you can never drift too far
away from the sphere of His love.

Loving God, protect me from the anger of my enemies.
Thank You that there is no end to Your love. Amen.

Find Strength in God

O LORD, be gracious to us; we long for
You. Be our strength every morning,
our salvation in time of distress.

Isaiah 33:2

Immediately after praying to God to save Israel, Isaiah describes Israel's distress: the Assyrians rejected their petition for peace, Lebanon was destroyed, and the plains of Sharon resembled a wilderness.

Isaiah's trust in God never faltered. He believed God's promises that He would preserve Israel and deliver His people. Because of this Isaiah could pray with confidence, "Be our strength every morning, our salvation in times of distress."

Like Isaiah, we can depend on God in times of distress and trouble. Call on Him in such times and feel the strength, that can only come from God, descend on you.

Omnipotent and omniscient God, help
me to trust in Your promises. Be my
strength and my salvation each day. Amen.

Answer God's Call

At that time men began to call
on the name of the LORD.

Genesis 4:26

There has never been a time in history when people have did not have a relationship with God. In our Scripture verse for today, people began to call on the name of God. They called on the name of the Lord because they needed someone to make sense of the bewildering and unsettling historical journey they had embarked upon.

Everything seemed to be beyond their strength; too overwhelming and drenched in mystery for their simple minds to fathom. By calling on God they found a Source strong enough to give them direction and help. We too can find God – by searching for Him and answering His call. We can do this through the guidance and strength of Jesus.

Holy God, grant me enough faith
to be able to answer Your call. Amen.

Let Jesus Guide You

Send forth Your light and Your truth,
let them guide me.

Psalm 43:3

How often have you experienced doubt, loneliness and anxiety? When an important decision has to be made do you find it difficult to make the right choice? If so, you are relying on your own limited insight instead of turning to God.

Regardless of the circumstances, put your plans, your doubts, your fears and your problems before the Lord's throne of grace and ask Jesus to be your Guide. Be sensitive to the whisperings and stirrings of the Holy Spirit in your life, and face the future with faith and hope. You can rest assured that the living Christ will be by your side, leading and guiding you.

Lord, let Your kindly light guide me. Help me to
understand that I should take life one day at a time
and seek Your guidance in everything I do. Amen.

Strength in His Power

Be strong in the Lord and in His mighty power.

Ephesians 6:10

In order to avoid feeling overwhelmed with anxiety and fear, uncertainty and inadequacy, it is essential to cling to Christ and draw your strength from Him. No one else but God knows you and your problems so intimately and completely, God loves you so much that He keeps a vigil of all-embracing love over you.

Armed with the assurance that you are supported and protected by the power, omnipotence, love and mercy of God, you should be equipped to deal with any situation that life might hand you.

Thank You for providing me with armor and shielding me against the shrewdness of Satan. You are my power and my strength. In You, Lord, I trust. Amen.

Productive Faith

He touched their eyes and said,
"According to your faith will it be done to you."

Matthew 9:29

There are people who regard faith as a mere commodity, something that you have a lot or very little of, depending on the circumstances.

You should, however, understand the importance and necessity of maintaining a disposition of expectation towards life. Only those who have an unfailing faith and trust in the Eternal God can face the future with courage and serenity. This great truth, and the acceptance of it in your life creates stability and enables you to face the future with confidence.

Help me Lord, to be steadfast in my faith
and to be forever devoted to Your work.
Bless me in abundance and help me
to use it to Your greater glory. Amen.

Faith Dispels Fear

He said to His disciples, "Why are you
so afraid? Do you still have no faith?"

Mark 4:40

There are few people who do not harbor fear in one form or another. It is a strange fact that many people cannot explain the fear that haunts them but it is nevertheless a burning presence in their lives.

There is only one sure cure for a life that is dominated by fear, and that is a living faith in Jesus Christ. Fear and faith cannot co-exist in the same life. Faith nurtures faith and fear nurtures fear. Place your trust in God.

At first, in the little things in your life, His love and wisdom will be revealed and confirmed, and in time, the bigger things in your life will be under His control, too.

As Your child, I know where to find veritable
peace. Dispel fear and selfishness from my
heart, so that I may serve You faithfully. Amen.

Confront Your Weaknesses

David found strength in the LORD his God.

1 Samuel 30:6

There are few people who can honestly say that they are equipped to meet and handle any situation with ease and confidence.

Regardless of what problems you face or how inadequate you might feel in any given situation – be it in the business world, on the home front, on the sports field, or even on a social level – you must surrender it in prayer to God. Ask Him to give you strength to handle the situation. Once you accept this and believe that He can and will do it, you can move forward with confidence in the knowledge that God's grace is sufficient to enable you to overcome your weaknesses.

Lord, even when I am filled with doubt; You are by my side.
You give me strength to overcome daily temptation,
so that one day I may behold Your splendor. Amen.

Walking with God

Noah was a righteous man, blameless among the
people of his time, and he walked with God.

Genesis 6:9

The quality of your life is largely dependent on the
company you keep. The vast majority of people are
influenced to a greater or lesser extent by the people
they associate with. Such an influence can be far-
reaching – negative as well as positive.

However, there is one influence that can bring
only good to your life, and that is the influence
of the Holy Spirit when you accept Christ as your
mentor. Because Jesus is the personification of God's
love, it goes without saying that in Him we are able
to find everything that is good, praiseworthy, true,
honorable, righteous, pure, virtuous and lovely.

Let your life be influenced by the living Christ.
Then your life will reflect those qualities that can
only come from God.

Forsaking all else, Lord Jesus, I open my life to the
influence of the Holy Spirit. Amen.

Steadfast in Faith

"Now be strong," declares the LORD, "and work.
For I am with you," declares the LORD Almighty.

Haggai 2:4

In the initial exciting phase of a person's born-again life, the Lord's work is done with zeal and enthusiasm. We are filled with the joy of a new life in Christ and we wish to share our feelings and ecstasy with others.

Whatever happens, do not succumb to the temptation to give up your work for Christ. Seek advice, help and guidance at all times but never allow discouragement to paralyze you in your honest pursuit to serve the Lord. Take courage and be steadfast in faith – through the mercy of Jesus Christ you will achieve success.

Your Creation, Lord, will never perish; it is everlasting.
Grant me the strength and make me Your servant
so that I may share in the fulfillment of Your will. Amen.

Only Jesus

When they looked up, they saw no one except Jesus.

Matthew 17:8

Perhaps it is time to pause for a while and examine your spiritual journey under the guidance of the Holy Spirit. Put all preconceived ideas aside and open up your spirit to His guidance.

It is the all-important sovereignty of Jesus Christ that generates a living faith in your heart. Faith is powerless and meaningless unless it is grounded in Christ and He rules as King in your life.

If you allow the Holy Spirit to work freely in your life, He will lead you into a more intimate relationship with Christ. Jesus will begin to occupy the central position in your life.

Desire of my heart, I thank You that my heart thirsts
for You all the time. Protect me from anyone
or anything that could draw me away from
experiencing Your presence in my life. Amen.

Grow in Christ

He is the image of the invisible God.

Colossians 1:15

Paul says that Jesus Christ and the eternal God are equal – that the One is like the Other.

This truth stirs one's soul, and you may feel that such spiritual heights are beyond your reach. Jesus lived on such a high moral level, setting examples of how to respond in certain situations, that you cannot live up to His example on your own. Yet this truth can also inspire and elevate us.

The living Christ does not condemn people for their sins, but inspires them to reach unprecedented heights. Depending on the strength and intensity of our devotion to Him, we can, in a small way, become like Jesus. And that is God's purpose for your life.

> Stand by me, Lord Jesus, help me to grow into
> the likeness of Your image through the power
> and guidance of the Holy Spirit. Amen.

Ensuring Growth

Make every effort to be found spotless,
blameless and at peace with Him.

2 Peter 3:14

The point of departure for any believer's spiritual lives is unconditional surrender to the love of Christ. Afterwards it is essential that we grow. A life starving for spiritual food will never fully develop.

You should care for your spiritual life by nourishing it with the Word of God. In addition you should be aware of the presence of the living Christ. This must happen every day so that He can guide your growth. His Spirit must reveal to you the true meaning of His eternal Word.

Pay serious attention to it and you will be surprised to discover that you are developing your full spiritual potential.

Master, help me to nourish my
spiritual life so that I will grow. Amen.

Spiritual Growth

Instead, speaking the truth in love, we will in all things grow up into Him who is the Head, that is, Christ.

Ephesians 4:15

Christianity without spiritual growth cannot bring true joy and satisfaction. When you received Christ into your life, you did not only accept a system of doctrines; you promised eternal faithfulness to Him because you believe in Him. You can only understand Him better if you share your life with Him, and stop focusing on yourself.

Growing in Christ is not an exercise meant to create a comfortable religious feeling far removed from the hard realities of life – it should rather inspire the believer to positive action.

Renew your prayer life; rediscover the Spirit of Christ in the Scriptures and see how growth in Christ will lead you to new dimensions of life.

Lord Jesus, make my faith a dynamic power through the renewal of my prayer life and Bible study. Amen.

Live for Christ

His divine power has given us everything we need
for life and godliness through our knowledge of Him
who called us by His own glory and goodness.

2 Peter 1:3

The call to live a Christian life rings out once again, but some of us are so overwhelmed by the intensity of the task that our faith falters because of our human weakness.

Yet we do not have to rely on our own abilities to serve God at all. Remember that Christ will not call you to any form of service without equipping you for it. He has set the example and all that He expects from you is to follow Him.

If you commit yourself to Him and place your trust in Him completely, He will provide you with everything that you need to truly live.

Heavenly Father, I dedicate myself to Your service anew,
in the certain knowledge that You will provide
everything that I need to live an abundant life. Amen.

Spiritual Maturity

When I was a child, I talked like a child, I thought
like a child, I reasoned like a child. When I became
a man, I put childish ways behind me.

1 Corinthians 13:11

Some people's spiritual journey can be compared
to a rocking horse: there is a lot of movement, but
little progress. They never achieve spiritual maturity
because they allow grudges to poison them with
bitterness. Allowing a grudge to fester could harm
your spirit and hinder your spiritual development.

Today you have an opportunity to grow by
God's grace, to put the negative behind you, and to
reach for a future of exuberant spiritual growth. If
you open your heart to the Holy Spirit's influence,
He will help you to forgive and forget – allowing
spiritual maturity.

Lord, I cannot do anything without You.
Fill me with Your Spirit so that I can grow
and experience fulfillment in You. Amen.

Growth Is Essential

I gave you milk, not solid food, for you were not
yet ready for it. For since there is jealousy and
quarreling among you, are you not worldly?

1 Corinthians 3:2-3

Many people believe that God is great and awesome. In faith they accept that He is love, but refuse to allow Him to fill their lives with that same love. He promised His power to all who serve Him, but they remain weak and powerless. They say they believe in Him, but they don't experience His loving presence.

The Christian way of life is meant to enrich the life of disciples. When you start becoming spiritually mature, you develop a greater love for others. When the love of Christ saturates you, negative attitudes such as pettiness, jealousy and strife are dissolved. And then you can rise above this immaturity and enjoy the solid food that the Holy Spirit gives.

Lord, I want to know more of Your love daily
so that I can love others in turn. Amen.

To Live for Christ

For to me, to live is Christ.

Philippians 1:21

Too many people live purposeless lives, passing through life with superficial goals. But this type of life cannot bring real satisfaction. Real joy and fulfillment come from having a goal in life that pleases Christ.

Your goal should be to live your life in God's grace, for His glory. You will not be a spiritual person only when the mood strikes you; your faith will remain constant in spite of your fluctuating emotions. Living for Christ means committing your spirit, soul and body to Him.

If you live for Christ, He will be alive to you and you will know the ecstasy of a life poured out before God as a thank-offering. Accept the gift of the Spirit in your life and allow Him to live through you. Then for you, to live is Christ and to die is gain.

Holy Jesus, live in me so that I will
do all things for Your glory. Amen.

A Growing Spirit

Your faith is growing more and more,
and the love every one of you
has for each other is increasing.

2 Thessalonians 1:3

If you are not enjoying your spiritual experience, you have probably allowed stagnation to rob you of your spiritual zest.

A vibrant and powerful spiritual life requires constant attention. There will never be a point when nothing more is required from you. The longer you walk with the Lord, the greater your enthusiasm should be, and any tendency to grow slack should be resisted with all your might.

Your quiet times nurture your spiritual life. When you start fading spiritually, ask God for the courage to confess your negligence and weakness, and to help you do something constructive about it.

Lord, You who are the True Vine, let me grow in You
so that I can bear fruit that will please You. Amen.

A Balanced Inner Life

If any of you lacks wisdom, he should ask
God, who gives generously to all without
finding fault, and it will be given to him.

James 1:5

Many people believe that to live a truly spiritual life, you need to live in seclusion; where the realities of life are either ignored or forgotten.

However, the lessons Jesus taught along the dusty roads of Palestine were very spiritual, yet essentially practical. For Him, everything – every thought and deed – was an expression of His relationship with His heavenly Father. Therefore, true Christians do not divide their lives into compartments, because all of their lives should be an expression of the spiritual.

Christianity touches the realities of every day and enables you to look, to a certain extent, at other people's problems as God does.

O Spirit, take control of my life and let everything I do
and say be an expression of my love for You. Amen.

Growth through Truth

You will grow as you learn to know
God better and better.

Colossians 1:10 NLT

If you ignore or undermine the necessity of growth in your spiritual life, it will not be long before you start to suffer on the stormy seas of disappointment and despair. There must be growth and development or your spiritual life will flounder on the rocks.

God makes resources available to us to assist us in our spiritual growth – fellowship with believers, Bible study and good deeds – but we should guard against these aids becoming goals in themselves. These are simply the result of our relationship with God.

There can only be spiritual growth if your main objective is to reflect the image of Christ more and more. This should be your heart's desire.

My Lord, let Your Holy Spirit take possession of
me so that I will live for Your glory alone. Amen.

Christlikeness

What will be has not yet been made
known. But we know that when
He appears, we shall be like Him.

1 John 3:2

The goal of every Christian should be to become like Jesus. Unconditionally accepting the lordship of Christ is the beginning of a new and satisfying way of life. Because you belong to Him, your love and mental and spiritual energy should be focused on becoming like Him.

Of course trying to do this in your own strength will only lead to frustration and disappointment. Pray that God will give you His Holy Spirit to help you with this process.

When you are united with Him, your faith becomes alive and your life is lived in obedience to Him. It will help you develop a Christlike character.

Master, I ask that You would fill me
with Your goodness so that I can be
completely obedient to You. Amen.

Maturity

Until we all reach unity in the faith and in
the knowledge of the Son of God, and
become mature, attaining to the whole
measure of the fullness of Christ.

Ephesians 4:13

It takes time for intellectual and spiritual maturity to reach its full potential.

In your efforts to reach maturity, you should have something against which to measure your progress. The apostle Paul teaches that we should measure our progress against nothing less than the character of Christ. Although this is an impossible goal, to aim any lower is to accept a secondhand life.

However, never forget Jesus' love for you and that He identifies with you in your human frailty. God will give you the strength to lead a godly life if you confess your dependence on Him every moment of the day. Draw daily from His strength.

Through Your strength, Master and Savior,
I can aim to follow in Your steps. Amen.

Christ in You

He said to them, "Go into all the world and
preach the good news to all creation."

Mark 16:15

Christians need to be witnesses for Christ. We must
not be ashamed of our faith in Jesus Christ. It is,
however, important to know when to speak and
when to be quiet.

There is one sure way to testify about your faith
without offending other people, and that is to follow
the example of Jesus Christ. His whole life was a
testimony of commitment to His duty, sympathy,
mercy, and love for all people – regardless of their
rank or circumstances. This is the very best way to be
a witness for Jesus.

Ask the Holy Spirit to guide you so that others
will see Christ in everything you do and say. In this
way you will fulfill the command of the Lord.

Help me, Lord Jesus, to let the Holy Spirit
live through me in such a way that others
may know of Your love for them. Amen.

Growth in Prayer

After Job had prayed for his friends, the LORD
made him prosperous again and gave
him twice as much as he had before.

Job 42:10

Making enemies isn't all that hard. But remember, it is possible to turn an enemy into a friend – although this isn't easy, as forgiveness requires true greatness.

Only those who have undergone meaningful spiritual growth can transform enmity into friendship. One sure and practical way to turn enemies into friends is to pray for them. This may sound absurd but it is a truly wise act if you desire a pleasant life. Prayer changes your attitude toward people and events, and when this happens, the battle is just about won. With God on your side you will have the ultimate victory.

Dear Lord, help me to grow in You so that I may develop
a forgiving spirit. Help me to follow Your example. Amen.

Stand by Your Convictions

> Simon Peter answered, "You are the
> Christ, the Son of the living God."
>
> *Matthew 16:16*

Many people long for a stronger faith. At one point or another we all need to answer the question that Jesus asked Simon Peter, "What about you? Who do you say I am?"

To benefit fully from the Christian experience, and to know the fullness and abundance of the true life that Jesus offers us, you must have a personal knowledge of the living Christ. This does not only mean learning everything about Him; it means acknowledging Him personally and surrendering your life to Him.

Acknowledge Christ's sovereignty over all creation and abundant life will be yours. That is why Jesus came to this world.

> Make me a prisoner of Your love, O Lord,
> because only then will I be truly free. Amen.

The Power of Inspired Thoughts

Above all else, guard your heart,
for it is the wellspring of life.

Proverbs 4:23

Our thoughts control our lives. If your spirit harbors thoughts of bitterness, hate and envy, your mind will be drenched with negative and destructive thoughts, and you will never experience the dynamism of the Christian faith.

By living in harmony with the living Christ, and allowing His Spirit to become an inspiration to your spirit, you can achieve the impossible. Embrace God's ways with joy, build a healthy and profound prayer life and engage in faithful Bible study. This will give your mind the inspiration and strength that is only experienced by those who have put Jesus Christ first in their lives.

Through Your enabling grace, Lord Jesus, my mind
is open to the inspiration of the Holy Spirit. Amen.

Desire God's Word

Direct my footsteps according to Your
word; let no sin rule over me.

Psalm 119:133

There are times in life when we long for guidance;
for someone who knows the road ahead, who can
help us avoid the potholes and dead-end streets.

This is the kind of desire that the psalmist had
for the Word of God – that it would lead him every
step of the way, and to true joy. In today's world it
often seems easier to desire God's freedom than His
commandments. But that is what brings true joy.

Reaffirm your desire for God's Word as your
guide today. Pray that God will help you resist the
specific sins that cause you to stumble often.

Lord of the Word, let Your commandments
guide me in the right paths. Amen.

Nourish Your Soul

"I am the bread of life. He who comes
to Me will never go hungry, and he who
believes in Me will never be thirsty."

John 6:35

In order to achieve a healthy existence and meet the demands of everyday life, food is essential.

Just as your physical body needs nourishment, so too does your spiritual life. It is an integral part of your existence on earth, as well as in eternity. Make sure that you maintain a sustained conversation with Christ so that you can constantly draw on the strength flowing from His everlasting reserves.

In this way you will ensure that your life will be powerfully enriched, because Jesus is living inside you through His Holy Spirit.

Lord, You are my daily bread and Your truth
sets me free. Thank You for presenting us with
the Word so that we may get to know You
better. Help me to find You therein. Amen.

Reach for the Sky!

I want to know Christ and the power of His
resurrection and the fellowship of sharing
in His sufferings, becoming like Him in
His death, and so, somehow, to attain
to the resurrection from the dead.

Philippians 3:10-11

Ambition is a commendable characteristic but there is one ideal in life that must overshadow all others: to live in the image of Christ. This must be the greatest ambition of every follower of Jesus.

The pure joy of a life in Jesus Christ cannot be measured. Such a life is priceless and precious. However, this demands a sacrifice. A sacrifice of your thoughts and ambitions must be laid on the altar of the living Christ so that His life can be reflected in you. The abundance of life in Him will be more than enough compensation for your complete surrender to your Savior and Redeemer.

Lord, I want to follow You and devote
my entire life to Your service. Amen.

Stand by Your Convictions

Do not conform any longer to the pattern
of the world, but be transformed
by the renewing of your mind.

Romans 12:2

There are a number of people who do not remain true to their principles and instead bow to societal pressure, suppressing their ideals.

If you do this, you violate your God-created character. What you believe is of crucial importance and becomes the only way for you to achieve true freedom in life.

If you are true to yourself, you may be scorned and rejected, but you will enjoy the satisfaction of knowing that you do not live a double life. It is only when you are at peace with yourself, and when you strive to please God rather than your fellow man, that you will be able to live a life of quality and contentment.

Bless our labor in You, Lord. Help us to be steadfast
and strong, filled with fervor towards You. Amen.

Grow in Wisdom

The fear of the LORD is the beginning
of wisdom; all who follow His precepts
have good understanding.

Psalm 111:10

To be educated is definitely an advantage in life. However, you can be highly educated and still suffer from spiritual want.

For the Christian, sanctification must always receive priority over education. A person who is in the process of developing spiritually is closer to the heart of God.

A spiritual person has discovered the true Source of wisdom in life. There is purpose in his service to God. He possesses peace and inner strength born from the fellowship of the Holy Spirit, and lives his life in such a way that he gains deep-rooted contentment and inspiration from it.

Lord, help me to spend every day in fellowship with
You and to experience the fullness of life. Amen.

Growth Requires Effort

The mind of sinful man is death, but the mind
controlled by the Spirit is life and peace.

Romans 8:6

Physical growth is nature's way of allowing your body
to develop. Your spiritual nature needs to grow, too.
Many people ignore this important aspect of their
lives because it cannot be observed or measured like
your body can. Yet, that does not make it any less
important.

The greatest Guide and Advisor that you could
ever find is Jesus Christ. He is the revelation of the
living God and therefore has a perfect understanding of the problems that you wrestle with. Having
a desire for oneness with Christ and yearning for a
deeper relationship with Him will result in spiritual
growth if you surrender to God completely.

I can do nothing without You. In You I can grow and
gain fulfillment. I wish to remain in You always. Amen.

Renewal Is Essential

Therefore we do not lose heart.
Though outwardly we are wasting away,
yet inwardly we are being renewed day by day.

2 Corinthians 4:16

From time to time it is necessary to take a break in order to refresh yourself and prevent burnout. Jesus often withdrew Himself from the masses so that He could be alone with His Father.

It is even more necessary for us to spend time with our heavenly Father. It is in those precious moments when you spend quiet time with God, that you will discover the work of the Holy Spirit in your life. He will fill the empty reservoirs of your life and you will return to the world refreshed, bearing testimony of Him with the new strength and energy that you have drawn from the Source.

Lord, fill me with Your Spirit. I ask for comfort,
strength and guidance – all to Your glory. Amen.

Reflect God's Glory

Be imitators of God, therefore, as dearly loved children.

Ephesians 5:1

Most of us have a role model we aspire to be like. Whether it is a teacher, a parent, an employer or even a friend, we want to be like them.

Yet, there is a much better role model for us, a perfect role model – Jesus Christ. Never forget that He lived and worked just like us and was subject to all the temptations, frustrations, joys and sorrows, which you and I are also subject to.

Allow the Holy Spirit to take control of your life and manage it in a way that is acceptable to God. Then you will display a measure of likeness to Christ that will glorify God.

Lord, transform me into Your image more and more.
Transfigure me so that I may become more like
You in my behavior, thoughts and words. Amen.

An Important Exercise

"The good man brings good things out of the good stored up in his heart, and the evil man brings evil things out of the evil stored up in his heart. For out of the overflow of his heart his mouth speaks."

Luke 6:45

It is the quality of your inner life, not that which you pretend to be, that is significant. For a while you may be able to present a false front, but a time will come when you will be put to the test.

Cultivating a practical spiritual life is the most important exercise that one can undertake. It influences every aspect of your life and creates moral stamina, which enables you to rise victoriously above inner weaknesses.

When you live in harmony with God and allow the Holy Spirit to work in you, you will experience a motivating force that will be reflected in your behavior.

Lord, teach me to fix my eyes on You more and more. I want to devote my whole life to You. Amen.

Whatever Is Noble

Finally, brothers, whatever is true, whatever is noble,
whatever is right, whatever is pure, whatever is lovely,
whatever is admirable – if anything is excellent or
praiseworthy – think about such things.

Philippians 4:8

Life can be an unpleasant or an exquisite experience, depending on your attitude towards it. When you are confronted with the cruelty of life, it is all too easy to allow it to affect your nature and character.

It requires spiritual sensitivity to consistently appreciate the beauty of life. To appreciate God as the Creator of all that is beautiful and noble, look around you. You will discover Him in unexpected places: in the smile of a friend, the innocence of a child, even a subtle act of love. In numerous ways, you will begin to see the wonder and beauty of life.

I bring You humble thanks, O Savior, that through
the presence of Your Spirit I can appreciate
the beauty and grandeur of life. Amen.

Share in His Life

God, who has called you into fellowship with
His Son Jesus Christ our Lord, is faithful.

1 Corinthians 1:9

God has called you to share in the life of His Son,
Jesus the living Christ – granting us a privilege
beyond words.

But with this privilege comes responsibilities.
Intimacy with the Father demands that the holy
characteristics of God must be revealed in your daily
life by love, honesty, selflessness and the integrity of
your purpose. If you walk in the truth of this amazing
grace, your understanding of God deepens and your
vision of what your life could be broadens.

Once you have this you will never again be limited
by secret fears and doubts. Instead you will face the
future with confidence in Christ.

You are the True Vine that gives lasting life.
Keep me safe, inspire me and bless me so
that I will forever remain fruitful. Amen.

Who You Can Become

However, as it is written: "No eye has seen, no ear has heard, no mind has conceived what God has prepared for those who love Him."

1 Corinthians 2:9

There are two sides to your personality: the person you are, and the person you would like to be. If these are in conflict with each other, you will experience bitter frustration and disappointment.

There is no harm in dreaming about the heights that you can possibly achieve, provided that you take steps to make your dream a reality. You have the potential for spiritual growth that is far beyond your wildest imaginings.

Spiritual greatness can be yours if you live in harmony with God. Your whole life should respond to His love with joy and gratitude.

I pray for inspiration and strength to become all that You created me to be. Help me to grow in You day by day and to fulfill Your vision for my life. Amen.

In the Service of God

Do your best to present yourself to God as one
approved, a workman who does not need to be
ashamed and who correctly handles the word of truth.

2 Timothy 2:15

Some people work tirelessly for God, seldom leaving any free time for themselves. Have you become so involved in God's work that you've lost sight of what God wants you to do?

If you don't get "topped up" by God regularly, one day something will just wither in your soul, all Christian activities will cease, and a life that may have been of great importance to God is lost.

The most important duty of any Christian worker is to strengthen your relationship with God every day. If you are too busy to spend time with Him in daily prayer then you are simply too busy to be an effective servant for Him.

Loving Master, help me not to lose sight
of the service You want me to do. Amen.

Renew Your Character

Therefore, if anyone is in Christ, he is a new creation;
the old has gone, the new has come!

2 Corinthians 5:17

Most people observe our characters and form an impression based on what they see. Yet, only a few people really take the time to develop an agreeable character.

Many people believe that a person's character cannot be changed. This is not true. If this were so, the redeeming love of Christ would have been in vain. Sinners can change into saints and unpleasant people can become amiable when the love of Christ enters their hearts.

When you open your life to Christ, His influence is reflected in your life and a transformation occurs. You surrender yourself to the Lord and through that, your character changes.

Your love is always with me, Lord. Father, draw
me closer into Your circle of love every day.
I want to remain in You. Amen.

It Is Well with My Soul

Why have you rejected us forever,
O God? Why does Your anger smolder
against the sheep of Your pasture?

Psalm 74:1

There are many people whose lives fall apart, and they feel abandoned and forsaken. Yet it is not true to believe that God will ever forsake you. He has promised to be with you always and to never leave you (Heb. 13:5). He even proved His unfathomable love by sacrificing His only Son on the cross for us.

God has a divine purpose for everything that happens in your life. Even when you are the victim of adversity, don't despair. He wants to use these negative circumstances to bring about His perfect will in your life.

Be still, my soul, the Lord is on your side.
Patiently bear all sorrow and grief and leave all
decisions in His loving hands. When everything
else fails, You, Lord, remain faithful. Amen.

Light in the Darkness

To those who have been called, who are loved
by God the Father and kept by Jesus Christ:
Mercy, peace and love be yours in abundance.

Jude 1-2

It seems as if the world is in a perpetual state of chaos. Lawlessness and violence are increasing, and people live in fear and insecurity. What is the solution to such a sad state of affairs?

There can only be one answer and that is to turn to Jesus Christ. He has already conquered this dark and hostile world and replaced fear with love so that you can confidently place your faith and trust in Him.

Believe in Jesus and His promises and He will give you the blessing of His peace that transcends all understanding. Trust in Him and He will lead you from the darkness into the light of His immeasurable love for humankind.

Thank You, my Lord and God, that You grant perfect
peace to Your children in this dark world. Amen.

God Is with You

The LORD your God is with you, He is mighty
to save. He will take great delight in you.

Zephaniah 3:17

When things go wrong in life it is easy to despair and become overwhelmed by a sense of complete helplessness and hopelessness.

If ever anything seemed hopeless, it was on the day of Jesus' crucifixion. The hopes and dreams of those who thought that He was the promised Messiah were shattered when He died on the cross. But then God intervened and miraculously turned apparent defeat into victory. The sorrowful Good Friday was transformed into the triumphant resurrection of the Easter Sunday – when Christ rose victoriously from the grave.

Whatever circumstances you might face, however dismal, always remember that God is with you and that He is in control.

Redeemer and Friend, thank You that I can be sure
that God loves me and is always with me. Amen.

Peace and Prosperity

You will keep in perfect peace him whose
mind is steadfast, because he trusts in You.

Isaiah 26:3

When our minds are focused on the love of God,
we experience indescribable peace of mind. When
you trust God during every day, and through every
problem, you will be able to enjoy His peace.

By focusing on Jesus Christ and the peace and
prosperity that He gives, you are set free from
worry because you know that God is in control of
your life – therefore no person or circumstance can
disturb your tranquility.

His love enfolds you and covers your loved ones as
well. This freedom cannot be taken away by anyone or
anything – simply because you put your trust in the
Lord Jesus Christ.

I want to trust You with every aspect of my life
because of Your great love. Then my heart will
be filled with peace and I will fear no evil. Amen.

Constructive Service

Being confident of this very thing,
that He who has begun a good work in you
will complete it until the day of Jesus Christ.

Philippians 1:6 NKJV

From every generation Jesus Christ has His followers who preach His gospel and do His will. Some of them reach high positions in society; others perform the task He has assigned to them to the best of their ability. One thing that the followers of Christ should understand is that the Master comes to them in their own, unique circumstances.

As your relationship with Jesus Christ deepens, you will be guided into constructive service. You become aware of a divine plan unfolding for your life. Such a plan might perhaps not be dramatic, but it is God's plan for you, and in executing it you will find joy and a deep satisfaction – as well as His protection.

Master, make my experience with You one that will take
me to higher heights in my walk with You. Amen.

Your Will Be Done

"Yet not My will, but Yours be done."

Luke 22:42

Many things come our way in life – unexpected disappointments and trials – and often we cannot see any reason for them. But whether they are major or minor problems, we need to handle them all.

The Lord's love for us is endlessly tender and encouraging. He wants us to trust where we cannot see, and it will not be a reckless leap in the dark, as sincere trust and faith says, "I know for certain that God's will is best for me."

This kind of faith leaves the choice up to God, with the words His Son taught us, "Your will be done!"

Eternal God and Father, thank You for sending
Your Son to come and teach me what it means
to let Your will be done in my life. Let
Your Spirit assist me in this. Amen.

Through His Strength

Blessed is the man who trusts in the
LORD, whose confidence is in Him.

Jeremiah 17:7

Everybody is searching for peace. No one can avoid the strain of life or the severe stress it brings with it. Jesus radiated love, serenity and peace; no matter how turbulent or chaotic the circumstances.

This was the result of His intimate relationship with His Father. Jesus regularly withdrew in solitude to pray and pour out His heart to His Father. Then He was able to return to a stormy life with the peace of heaven in His heart.

Whatever life may have in store for you, you will be victorious in His strength because, "I can do everything through Him who gives me strength" (Phil. 4:13).

You are my Keeper, O Lord. I place myself
under Your control and in Your care. That
is why I am assured of Your peace. Amen.

The Great Comfort

He comforts us in all our troubles
so that we can comfort others.

2 Corinthians 1:4 NLT

Paul had first-hand knowledge of the Father's compassion during his trials. He learnt that God is "the source of all comfort" (see 2 Cor. 1:3). This comfort flows directly from our fellowship with God.

It often happens that our own sorrow is relieved while we comfort others. Our hearts become sensitive to others because of the trials and sorrow we have wrestled with ourselves. That is why there is a blessing in every burden in our lives. We must simply receive the grace through the Holy Spirit to see it and share it with others. In so doing, our own sorrow is toned down and we are able to reach out to others with a comforting hand and heart.

Holy Comforter, let Your healing love enfold
my heart so that I will be tender
in my contact with others' grief. Amen.

Peace Amidst Chaos

In keeping with His promise we are
looking forward to a new heaven and
a new earth, the home of righteousness.

2 Peter 3:13

In times of crises many people tend to collapse in defeat against what they perceive to be impossible problems. But to everyone who believes in Him, Jesus offers a life of abundance.

The Lord offers you His Holy Spirit if you surrender yourself to Him. It is His Spirit who gives you the ability to handle life's problems successfully. Whatever your circumstances may be, remember that Jesus is constantly at your side, guiding you and helping you. Place your trust in Him as He leads you, and remember that He is guiding you toward God's eternal kingdom where there is only harmony and peace.

Beloved Guide, I know that this life's struggles and
problems will soon pass, and then I will enter
into the eternal peace of Your kingdom. Amen.

Peace in the Storm

While they were still talking about this,
Jesus Himself stood among them and
said to them, "Peace be with you."

Luke 24:36

The stress, horror and inner conflict we may experience in life causes our peace to disappear, leaving us moody and discontent.

That is why we need to develop inner reserves from which to draw strength in difficult situations. When things go wrong and stress starts to overwhelm you, purposefully refuse to be swept into its current. Guard against bad temper and irritability.

Deliberately choose to remain tranquil by controlling your thoughts. Spend some time in God's presence, reaffirm your dependence on Him, and soon your spirit will become calm and His peace will refresh your life.

Eternal God who gives me peace in Jesus Christ,
lead me to quiet waters where there is peace
in the midst of the bustle of life. Amen.

I Know for Certain

He will never leave you nor forsake you.

Deuteronomy 31:6

It is important to have someone you can rely on and turn to in times of trouble. Yet sometimes even the closest friends can disappoint you.

Our Lord and Master will never let us down though. If you need comfort, the Lord will comfort you. If you need guidance, the Lord will guide you. If you need inspiration for a difficult task, the Lord will inspire you.

If the road ahead of you seems to be strewn with problems, concerns and troubles, then ask the Lord to help you and you will discover that He is as faithful as His Word promises.

God my Father, thank You that I have the
assurance that You will never leave me nor
forsake me. Forgive me for the times when
I've failed and disappointed You. Amen.

Take Your Worries to God

Do not be anxious about anything,
but in everything, by prayer and petition,
present your requests to God.

Philippians 4:6

Many people like to sit and brood over their problems. If we do this, we allow worry to flourish and then we lose hope.

Write down your worries clearly and simply. Then calmly pray about each one and scale them down to their real size. Prayerfully confirm that God is in control of every situation and that worry will no longer affect your tranquility and peace of mind.

The secret is to take your burdens to God in prayer. If you take this step today you will discover that you are prohibiting worry and anxiety from clouding your future because you will discover that Christ is all-sufficient for your needs, today and tomorrow.

Savior, I praise and thank You that You protect
me and lead me into a pleasant future. Amen.

Peace in the Storm

"Be still, and know that I am God."

Psalm 46:10

If you allow your thoughts to dwell on the things that are happening in the world today, you run the risk of being caught up in a whirlpool of hatred, bitterness and fear.

Yet, when your faith threatens to falter, God gives you the power to believe that all things will work out for the good of those who love Him. Peace is the direct result of trust.

When your faith in God is sure, you receive an inner calm that brings balance to your life. Put God first in all things and you will know His peace and joy, even in the most trying circumstances.

Almighty God, thank You that with You at
the center of my life I fear no storms, not even
problems as threatening as hurricanes. Amen.

Heavenly Peace

"Peace I leave with you; My peace I give you."

John 14:27

The peace that Jesus offers His followers differs from human peace and allows us to look at life through God's eyes. When we do this, the worldly things suddenly do not seem to be that important. What God thinks of you, and how you relate to God, forms the foundation for your peace.

We need His peace in our everyday lives as well as in our inner beings. The Lord does not want us to stress about what is happening around us. So in all the confusion and chaos of daily life, look away from the world and look up to God. He is waiting to grant us His peace and love.

Father God, thank You that I know for certain
that You have not only redeemed me, but that
You also grant me Your heavenly peace. Amen.

God's Peace Is Unfailing

Who is God besides the LORD?
And who is the Rock except our God?

2 Samuel 22:32

Often when people are experiencing problems, or if they need advice, they turn to a friend for help. But human effort always falls short.

If you find yourself in a difficult situation, don't underestimate the power and love of God. Complete healing flows from an absolute and unconditional trust in, and surrender to, the living Christ. It doesn't matter what your problem is, the only lasting solution is to be found in the unfathomable love which God, through Jesus, bestowed on humanity.

Never be too proud or too afraid to turn to Jesus. Lay all your problems at His feet. He gave His life for you and will grant you the healing balm of His peace.

I want to hold on to You, Lord, when the storm winds blow and I feel insecure. Grant me Your peace. Amen.

Peace Be with You!

For the sake of my brothers and friends,
I will say, "Peace be within you."

Psalm 122:8

The world has enough problems of its own without us adding to them by engaging in bitter quarrels and harboring hurts against others. To enjoy life fully, it is essential that you live in peace with your fellow man – but you can only do that if you have peace within yourself.

During His earthly ministry, Jesus had to handle a tremendous amount of adversity. He endured mockery, hatred, humiliation, unfair criticism and rejection. But, He never allowed circumstances to get the better of Him.

This was only possible because He was at peace with God, with Himself, and with all people. Accept it and express it through your life and you will experience a life of harmony and peace.

Savior, because I found You, my life is
filled with an indescribable peace. Amen.

Turn to Christ

The LORD gives strength to His people;
the LORD blesses His people with peace.

Psalm 29:11

Few people can honestly say that they do not long for peace of mind and inner tranquility. The troubles and pressures of life can drive many to seek comfort in different things; be it tranquilizers, drugs, professional help or even alcohol. Others simply give in to despair and just go through the motions of life.

The only proven way to handle the problems and tensions of life is by having a faith that is steadfastly grounded in the living Christ. Hold on to Him in all circumstances, talk to Him and, regardless of how desperate your situation might be, trust that He is always with you. His peace will then fill your heart, helping you overcome all your fears.

Prince of Peace, please help me to turn to You first
in everything that happens to me today. Amen.

Your Search for Peace

To whom He said, "This is the resting place,
let the weary rest"; and, "This is the place
of repose" – but they would not listen.

Isaiah 28:12

People today struggle with tremendous pressure and in such stressful times tend to become very weary and exhausted.

That is why Christ invites us by saying, "Come to Me, all you who are weary and burdened, and I will give you rest" (Matt. 11:28). Yet, instead of accepting this offer, many of us still try to find man-made solutions to our problems in our own strength.

Regardless of how busy you are, you must make time to withdraw from the demands of the day and spend time quietly at the feet of the Master. Focus on Him and His love. Regardless of how demanding and frantic your life may be, in the quietness you will be strengthened by God's peace.

I have such a need for Your rest, Lord. Help me to be strengthened in the peace of Your presence. Amen.

Freedom in Christ

Jesus replied, "I tell you the truth,
everyone who sins is a slave to sin."

John 8:34

Many people are slaves to destructive habits and lead sinful lives that are devoid of beauty and liberty.

Unfortunately many people have accepted this bondage as a way of life. They are content to live an inferior spiritual life because they are oblivious to the freedom and peace that Christ offers.

When you accept Christ as your Lord, you enjoy a new freedom, and a new pattern of life begins. All bitterness dissipates in His glorious love. The Holy Spirit sanctifies your thoughts, words and actions. The freedom that Christ gives spans your whole life and is the only way to find freedom and joy.

By doing Your will, Father, my life will be
filled with a peace that lasts forever. Amen.

Christ's Peace – My Inheritance

Let the peace of Christ rule in your hearts.

Colossians 3:15

This world's peace is a poor reflection of the peace that God gives to His children. The peace of God is the most wonderful peace imaginable. It affects every area of our lives. It is constant and does not change according to our moods.

But this peace requires a steadfast faith in Jesus Christ, who is the Source of this peace. Such peace banishes worry, because that is the weapon the devil uses to undermine our peace. Jesus prohibits fear, because fear is the enemy of all peace.

I praise and thank You, Lord, for the peace that conquers the fear and anxiety in my life. Amen.

God's Perfect Timing

"I am the LORD; in its time I will do this swiftly."

Isaiah 60:22

Very often we find it difficult to accept God's timing, but we must never get impatient with the fact that He does not always react when we want Him to.

It is wrong to try to subject the omniscient God to your timetable. We only see the circumstances and problems that weigh us down now, while God sees the bigger picture from an eternal perspective. God's timing is always perfect, even though it may not seem that way to you now.

When His will becomes our primary concern, then we will start to understand God's perfect timing and will no longer be subject to fits of anxiety caused by circumstances.

Lord, You are omnipresent. When I lose all
hope, You are there. Thank You that I may
know that my life is safe in Your hands. Amen.

Control Your Thoughts

Great peace have they who love Your law,
and nothing can make them stumble.

Psalm 119:165

Your thoughts influence your deeds. It is therefore imperative to discipline your thoughts in order to have a positive disposition towards life.

The greatest force in a healthy and emotional life is allowing the Holy Spirit to take control of your thoughts. You can, through the strength that Christ grants you, control your thoughts, and in doing so, experience the peace of God. There will be moments of disruption when evil thoughts will try to re-establish themselves, but if you focus on God and give Him control, nothing will destroy your peace.

You are my only Savior. Help me to trust in
God as my shield against the Evil One. Amen.

The Blessing
of a Peacemaker

"Blessed are the peacemakers, for
they will be called sons of God."

Matthew 5:9

Peacemakers create healthy relationships. They are people in whose presence bitterness, hatred and unforgiveness simply cannot survive. They are children of God and aim to be at peace with all people.

To live in peace with friends is easy, but what about your enemies? Therefore it is peace at a risk: it includes peace with your enemies and persecutors.

Peacemakers are willing to venture something so that they can perform a deed of peace for the sake of Christ. To be a peacemaker is not a pious ideal or an unreachable dream; in Christ, it is an achievable goal through the help of the Holy Spirit.

Holy Spirit of God, enable me, for the sake of Jesus,
my Lord, to be a peacemaker in this world. Amen.

In His Safekeeping

He led His own people like a flock of sheep,
guiding them safely through the wilderness.
He kept them safe so they were not afraid.

Psalm 78:52-53 NLT

On a spiritual level, a life of doubt, anxiety and fear without any peace of mind can become a real nightmare. If you want peace and tranquility to become a reality in your life, it is of the essence that you cling to your faith in Jesus.

Believe in His promise that He will always be with you and never let you down (see Heb. 13:5). Go to Him with every situation that makes you anxious and trust Him to protect you against all fear, anxiety and evil. Then you will experience the peace of God.

Place yourself in God's safekeeping now and forever. Rest assured that He will keep you safe.

Protect me, Lord, in all circumstances and keep
me safe so that I will overcome my fear. Amen.

Green Pastures

He makes me lie down in green pastures,
He leads me beside quiet waters.

Psalm 23:2

It is a blessed assurance to know that an omnipotent and loving God guides you from day to day. The Lord does not promise that all the pastures will always be green – sometimes they will be barren and desolate. He has also not promised that the waters will always be tranquil – sometimes the waves will break turbulently over us and the sky will be covered with ominous storm clouds. But the promise is that God, in His time, will bring us to green pastures and quiet waters.

If we put our childlike and unconditional trust in Him, we may rest assured in the knowledge that God will guide us in our everyday lives.

Lord Jesus, Shepherd of my life, thank You that
I may be safe and secure in Your care. Help me
to accept Your guidance at all times. Amen.

The Lord Guides Us

Then the disciple whom Jesus
loved said to Peter, "It is the Lord!"

John 21:7

When the disciples beached at dawn following a night of fishing, they recognized Jesus on the shore. He had prepared a meal for them. This tells us of the Lord's care – even after His resurrection He stayed close to His children.

We will get rid of a multitude of anxieties and confusions if we only recognize the Lord's hand in our lives and know for certain that He is by our side in every situation.

We know that He guides us on the path that is best for us. If we meet Jesus with unfailing certainty every day on our path through life, then we are amongst the most fortunate of all people on earth.

*I praise and glorify You, Lord Jesus, because I see
Your hand in every situation in my life and I know
for certain that You will never forsake me. Amen.*

The Source of Peace

I pray that God, the source of hope,
will fill you completely with joy and
peace because you trust in Him.

Romans 15:13 NLT

Peace of mind is the quiet but certain knowledge that you are secure in God's care. When I accept God as the Source of my peace and joy, and I become inseparably united with Him, I have taken the first step on the road to peace.

Few things can destroy peace of mind as completely as strife in your relationship with God and those around you. To remedy this situation, our relationship with God needs to be strengthened through Jesus Christ and the Holy Spirit. The wonder of God's peace is one of the "perks" of a surrendered life. The condition for this is faith.

Merciful Father, thank You that I can draw
near to You, the Source of true peace. Amen.

Shelter from the Storm

He who dwells in the shelter of the Most High
will rest in the shadow of the Almighty. I
will say of the LORD, "He is my refuge and
my fortress, my God, in whom I trust."

Psalm 91:1-2

Our lives can only be safe if we trust in the Most High. His protection is not limited to certain times of the day; rather we are under God's protection every moment of the night and day.

You need not fear anything – not the dangers of night or the attacks of day, not illness and plague, nor war and fighting. God is with us everywhere. With His protection and presence you will be able to conquer all dangers.

Take shelter under God's wings and be assured that you have a safe refuge where true peace and safety can be found.

God of Ages, Your children have always found
shelter and protection in You. Thank You
that I know where my safety lies. Amen.

Feast of Peace

God is not a God of disorder but of peace.

1 Corinthians 14:33

In a world that is so chaotic and conflicted, it seems naively idealistic to talk about peace. But peace is one of the gifts that God offers us through Jesus Christ. It is an eternal truth that all who love and serve God will experience His peace in their personal lives.

For those who have God's peace, it does not mean that they will escape the problems and sorrows of life, it means that they possess something more precious than the spirit of the times in which we live.

Christ's peace is not a passive quality that shuts our eyes to the harsh reality, but creates a positive approach to life, based on the belief in the trustworthiness of God.

Praise the Lord! Jesus, You came to bring
peace. Thank You for the peace of this
glorious truth ruling in my own heart. Amen.

Relieve Anxiety

"Do not worry about tomorrow, for
tomorrow will worry about its own things.
Sufficient for the day is its own trouble."

Matthew 6:34

In times of pressure and stress – when it feels as if hope is dying – anxiety takes root in your heart and mind and flourishes. Anxiety is the product of a confused mind and little faith.

One way of overcoming a feeling of anxiety is to determine its cause. For many people their anxiety is vague and indefinable, but it continues to erode their spirit and mind – with disastrous consequences. Take your anxieties to God and ask Him to be Master of the situation. If you do this, you are no longer allowing the Devil to attack your calm approach to life or allowing anxiety to spoil tomorrow.

Holy Spirit of God, help me not to be anxious
about tomorrow, because You have every
day in Your eternal and loving hand. Amen.

A New Hope

Trust in the LORD with all your heart and
lean not on your own understanding.

Proverbs 3:5

The decisions you make today could have far-reaching consequences for your life. Spend some time in God's presence today and seek His will. This will lay a solid foundation for a life built on trust in Christ. God will never disappoint you. Through the Holy Spirit, He will open up new horizons of what life can offer.

The more closely you walk with Him, the more clearly you will understand all that He can do in and through your life. Resolve to strengthen and enrich your relationship with Christ so that you can blossom and be as fruitful as He desires you to be.

Loving Lord, I come before You in earnest
prayer, asking that my imperfect life might
reflect something of Your holiness. Amen.

Hope for the Future

Has He not made with me an everlasting
covenant, arranged and secured in every part?

2 Samuel 23:5

Many people look to the future with deep anxiety because they are carrying the heavy burden of their daily responsibilities alone. Unless you have a strong faith, this could have far-reaching effects on your physical, emotional and mental well-being.

The Son of the Most High God died and rose from the dead to set you free from this burden of worry. God loved you so much that Jesus Christ gave His life to redeem you from the terrible burden of anxious worries. Unlike those who have no hope, you are blessed with the assurance that the Savior died in order that you may live. Regardless of the circumstances you're in, this assurance should be a great comfort and encouragement.

I thank You, Lord, that in spite of my
circumstances I can praise You, for You are
in control and You are ever-faithful. Amen.

Living Hope

Praise be to the God and Father of our Lord
Jesus Christ! In His great mercy He has given
us new birth into a living hope through the
resurrection of Jesus Christ from the dead.

1 Peter 1:3

Let your anxious heart rejoice with the glorious expectations of all the riches and treasures that await you in heaven. Thank God for such a hope and turn your thoughts away from all the burdens and worries of the world. Renew your mind with thoughts of the pure untainted inheritance that is waiting for you – an inheritance that can never be taken away or destroyed.

Prayer focuses our hearts on heaven while our feet remain firmly planted on the earth. So even if you are involved in a bitter struggle here on earth, remember your inheritance in heaven and praise the Lord for it.

I thank and praise You, Holy God, for all the treasures
that You have set aside for me in heaven. Amen.

Trust God

I heard, but I did not understand. So I asked,
"My lord, what will the outcome of all this be?"

Daniel 12:8

People often find it difficult to understand God's purpose for their lives – especially when things go wrong. Their vision of the future fades and their faith starts to waver.

The core of a strong faith depends on your ability to trust God completely, no matter what happens. The true test of faith comes when things turn against you; when you are tempted to question God; when you are in total despair.

Jesus had an unconditional trust in God. Even in His darkest moments, His faith was strong enough to enable Him to fulfill the will of the Father. Trust God in all circumstances and the grace of God will help you deal with every situation.

Lamb of God, I look up to You to strengthen my faith
through the work of Your Holy Spirit in my life. Amen.

Trust in God

Though an army besiege me, my heart
will not fear; though war break out
against me, even then will I be confident.

Psalm 27:3

Like never before, people are worried and anxious about what the future holds. It is essential for people to have a spiritual foundation upon which to base their hopes and expectations.

Unless you have a positive trust in a power greater than yourself, the future will be filled with uncertainty for you.

Faith in God must be intimate and personal if it is to give you hope for the future. The omnipotent Creator God has not abandoned this world despite appearances to the contrary. His master plan will still be carried out, just place your trust in Him and meet the future with the serenity He will give you.

Savior and Lord, I live from day to day trusting Your
very real presence and omnipotence in this world.
I do not fear because You are my refuge. Amen.

On Eagles' Wings

Those who hope in the LORD will renew their strength. They will soar on wings like eagles.

Isaiah 40:31

Too often we get hung up on things that don't really matter and we allow them to distort our view of life.

A positive Christian, however, has the ability to rise above small irritations by trusting in the Lord in all circumstances and by always remaining conscious of His presence. It is impossible to be trivial and small-minded when the love of Christ fills your heart and mind.

Spreading God's love by the power of the Holy Spirit means being able to rise above trivialities and reach the heights that the God of love desires from all His children. Then we can rise up on the wings of eagles and see things from their true perspective.

Holy Spirit, fill me with Your presence and help me to trust in God so I can rise above my problems. Amen.

Unshakable Trust

Be joyful in hope, patient in affliction.

Romans 12:12

When everything seems to be going wrong you may feel overwhelmed by your problems and want to give up or try to solve them in your own strength. But remember, the Lord has promised to never leave nor forsake you.

However, you must have patience because you cannot hurry or prescribe to God. He does everything in His own perfect time and in His own perfect way. God sees the big picture of your life – He is all-knowing and all-seeing.

Ask the Holy Spirit to teach you to wait patiently on the Lord. Then, with childlike trust, you can leave everything in God's hands. Those who stand steadfast in affliction receive God's most precious gifts from His treasure house of mercy.

Lord and Father, I find peace of mind
in trusting You completely. Amen.

Holy and Omniscient

The LORD has established His throne in
heaven, and His kingdom rules over all.

Psalm 103:19

In adverse circumstances, people often start to
doubt God's power and majesty. Their faith wanes
and the obstacles of life cause them to stumble.

When you find yourself surrounded by difficulties, hold on to your faith and put all your trust
in the victorious Christ. In all the centuries since
Creation, there has not been one instance where the
righteousness of God did not triumph over evil.

This same God wants to be your daily companion. He reigns supremely over everything and
everyone. Let this be your source of strength and
power in life, with all its problems and demands.

Father, I find strength and inspiration in
knowing that You are with me, and that Your
righteousness prevails in every situation. Amen.

Facing the Future

"I know the plans I have for you," declares the LORD,
"plans to prosper you and not to harm you."

Jeremiah 29:11

If you are fearful and worried about the future, you will project the very things that you fear and wish to avoid, into your future. Like Job you will then find yourself saying, "What I feared has come upon me" (Job 3:25).

A sure way of increasing your hope is to work hard at maintaining a positive faith in Jesus Christ. Strengthen the ties that you have with Him until He becomes a living, dynamic reality to you.

The more real He becomes to you, the more your fears, which have undermined your trust in Him, will be transformed into a steadfast, constant faith in the Lord. Then you will be able to venture fearlessly into the future.

Holy Master, give me hope and confidence
in the future as I walk with You. Amen.

Trust God

"I am the LORD your God who takes hold of your right
hand and says to you, 'Do not fear; I will help you.'"

Isaiah 41:13

Every follower of Jesus faces days where his or her
spiritual life seems mediocre and their enthusiasm is
dampened by indifference.

If this is you, then you need a fresh experience
with God to drive the darkness from your life. No
matter how your feelings change, God's love for you
remains steadfast. He loves you with an everlasting,
unceasing love, and, even though you feel far from
Him, He is always close to you.

One of the benefits of going through dark times
in life is to appreciate the light and sunshine of God's
love when we experience it once again. God is able
to use even the darkest experiences on your earthly
pilgrimage to the benefit and blessing of others.

Please hold my hand, Lord. I know that You will
lead me into the future one step at a time. Amen.

A Life Based on Trust

I have learnt to be content whatever the
circumstances. I know what it is to be in
need, and I know what it is to have plenty.

Philippians 4:11-12

As a follower of Christ you have powers at your
disposal that enable you to tackle life positively and
constructively. Remember that dynamic discipleship
is based on faith that finds expression in deeds, not
in feelings. Focus on the fact that God loves you,
even though you might be experiencing the darkest
time of your life.

Acknowledge the fact that He will never leave you,
even though you may not be able to feel His presence
right now. If your life is based on your faith in Christ,
your confidence will increase and you will overcome
every feeling of inferiority. There will be no situation
that you will not be able to handle through Christ's
wisdom and power.

I thank You, Lord Jesus, that I can start every day with
confidence because I find my strength in You. Amen.

Faith Requires Trust

"Master, we've worked hard all night and
haven't caught anything. But because
you say so, I will let down the nets."

Luke 5:5

The disciples had labored hard throughout the night without catching any fish. They were experienced fishermen and knew there were no fish to catch. Yet, at Jesus' words, they let down the nets once more. According to the Scriptures they caught so many fish that the nets began to tear. And so their faith was rewarded.

When you lay a matter before God you should trust Him so much that you are willing to accept His will and be obedient to the prompting of His Spirit no matter what. Forget about what others think or say; trust God. He will reward your faith.

I place my trust in You completely, Lord Jesus,
in the knowledge that You will never
disappoint me. Help me not to disappoint
You through my unbelief. Amen.

Hold Fast to Hope

Let us hold unswervingly to the hope we
profess, for He who promised is faithful.

Hebrews 10:23

Sometimes everything in your life looks hopeless
and bleak. Your dreams have been destroyed, your
hope has died, and nothing seems to be working out
right. In such a depressed state we become easy prey
to the Devil, whose main aim is to drive a wedge
between our heavenly Father and us.

When you feel dejected, remember that Jesus has
promised to be by your side throughout your life.
He invites you to cast your problems on Him and to
trust Him in times of distress. Study the Gospels, see
how compassionate and loving Jesus was towards
people, and draw hope and comfort from that.

Thank You, Lord Jesus, that even when I feel dejected,
You are always by my side. Lift me from the well of
misery and let me sing a song of praise once more. Amen.

The Richness of Life

Not that we are competent in ourselves
to claim anything for ourselves, but
our competence comes from God.

2 Corinthians 3:5

If you are searching for the deeper meaning of life, you are on an exciting journey. Fix your eyes beyond the temporal, and discover that you are an eternal being created in God's image.

God gives purpose to your days and motivation to live life to the full. As you yield to the control of the Holy Spirit, you will become more and more aware of how magnificent life truly is.

If we would only surrender to God without restraint we would see His glory and omnipotence and we would experience the richness of life in all its facets.

Great and mighty God. I praise You for revealing Your
greatness to me and enriching my life through it. Amen.

Peace through Jesus Christ

He came and preached peace to you who were
far away and peace to those who were near.

Ephesians 2:17

Christ is the source of our peace. He made peace
with God possible for us: "Therefore, since we
have been made right in God's sight by faith, we
have peace with God because of what Jesus Christ
our Lord has done for us" (Rom. 5:1). The unique
relationship of peace between Creator and creature
became possible through Christ's sacrificial death.

When it seems as if there is no order in your
life, remember that Christ's peace creates order
from chaos. Then your peace need not rely on your
feelings, emotions or state of mind, but on your
relationship with God through Jesus Christ. He is,
after all, the source of all genuine and lasting peace.

Holy Lord Jesus, my salvation and peace are found
in You alone. Let this certainty remain the mainstay
of my peace, calm and undying hope. Amen.

Light in Darkness

Even in darkness light dawns for the upright, for the
gracious and compassionate and righteous man.

Psalm 112:4

Every believer knows that there will be times when
dark clouds of affliction come. At first God is such a
glorious reality to you and joy floods your life, but
the clouds of despondency soon appear.

When that happens, it is essential to re-establish
the truth that God is unchanging; His love for you
is exactly what it has always been. You may find the
darkness hard to accept and God may seem far off,
but hold on steadfastly to the assurance that God
loves you and that He cares for you.

Fortunately the dark times do end and you will
step out of the shadows with new strength and walk
in God's sunshine again.

I will trust You in the darkness, because
I know that You are good. Amen.

Plan with God

So that your faith might not rest on
men's wisdom, but on God's power.

1 Corinthians 2:5

Have you ever experienced the disappointment of seeing carefully planned dreams fall apart? Many people who experience such a setback are unwilling to take any other risks.

Don't let that happen to you – don't let your potential lie wasted and unused. When you trust God in everything you do and submit to His will and obey Him, you might feel that things move too slowly for you, but be patient. Steadfastly put your trust in God and you will find peace of mind knowing that God is in control and that the fulfillment of His plans will be to your lasting benefit.

Lord, I know that when I bring my plans for my life
to You, You will show me what Your plans are, and
You will help me to succeed in all things. Amen.

God's Presence

At this, Abram fell face down in the dust. Then God
said to him, "This is My covenant with you."

Genesis 17:3-4 NLT

Abraham didn't respond to God's declaration by
saying, "That's fine with me, Lord. From now on we
walk together, hand in hand." He knew that he was
in the presence of the Almighty, Sovereign God. He
fell on his face in reverence for God, in speechless
worship; in this way acknowledging that God is the
Sovereign Authority in the universe. This response
was also an indication that he submitted himself to
God and to God's covenant.

The Almighty God is not something you keep in
your pocket and take out when you have no one else
to talk to. He is the Creator God, the King of kings. Be
humble and respectful and react to His commands
with worship and submission.

Heavenly Father, You are the Almighty Creator, the King
of kings. None can compare with You. Amen.

Your Divine Companion

The righteous cry out, and the LORD hears
them; He delivers them from all their troubles.

Psalm 34:17

Many people struggle with loneliness for a variety
of reasons. When you find yourself feeling depressed
and lonely, Satan will try to sow seeds of doubt,
discouragement and despair in your heart, making
you want to give up hope.

But don't give up! The hand of God rests on you
always. Rather lay your fears and worries at the feet
of the living Christ. Open up your heart and life to
the Holy Spirit and He will fan the flame of hope
once more, allowing it to burn brightly and light
your path.

Powerful Redeemer, grant me the strength to
keep my hand firmly in Yours even under the
most difficult circumstances. Lead me from
the darkness into Your wonderful light. Amen.

Light up Your Life

When Jesus spoke again to the people,
He said, "I am the light of the world.
Whoever follows Me will never walk in
darkness, but will have the light of life."

John 8:12

Darkness can cause fear, depression, loneliness and sorrow. The darkness of the soul has a similar effect on people. When light comes, it brings relief and a feeling of safety.

The light of hope and peace flickers and dims when we face afflictions and trials. The only way to overcome the darkness is to turn to Christ. Instead of fearing the darkness, light a small candle of faith to brighten it.

Walk in His light and soon you will find that the darkness has passed. With His light in your heart, each day becomes radiant for you.

Loving Guide, while You hold my hand I am safe
and secure. Strengthen my faith daily. Amen.

On the Way with Christ

They asked each other, "Were not our hearts burning within us while He talked with us on the road and opened the Scriptures to us?"

Luke 24:32

Quiet moments spent in the presence of God are precious. During these moments you draw inner strength from Him and your spirit is united with His. Unfortunately, at times when we are busy, it can easily happen that we neglect our quiet times.

However, when you have met with God you will find it easier to concentrate on Him during those busy times when your thoughts are in turmoil and storms rage around you. Use such moments to confirm His presence and acknowledge His authority in your life. You will then experience the joy of His closeness and Christ will be your Companion and Leader every day that you walk life's road.

Please help me, O Lord, to be aware of
Your presence every moment of the day, and
in this way strengthen the bond between us. Amen.

God Is Faithful

The LORD always keeps His promises;
He is gracious in all He does.

Psalm 145:13

All of us, at one point or another, when faced with a certain situation feel hopeless and defeated.

Yet whatever the predicament you are in, however dark the outlook, never underestimate the extent of God's love for you and the expanse of His grace. Look at examples in the Bible or in history when God transformed despair into hope and defeat into victory through His grace.

He is waiting for you to turn to Him and trust in Him. Your faith will be rewarded and, in His own wonderful way, He will deliver you.

God, through the years You have proved Yourself
to be faithful. Therefore I will hold on to Your hand
in the future and trust in You. Amen.

Love Fills the Heart with Hope

Brothers, we do not want you to grieve
like the rest of men, who have no hope.

1 Thessalonians 4:13

Hope and despair are found in the hearts of people and not in circumstances. Love is so important because it causes hope to triumph. When things are at their darkest, hope rises through love to light the darkness of night. There is no room for despair; God has enough love to avert it. He has woven hope into the nature of man so that we can trust in the future.

When all is hopeless, it is hope that keeps us going. Hope strengthens the soul so that we can hold on to eternity and on to the love of God. His love is infinite; He gives us hope out of love.

Lord, may I never believe that anyone
is hopelessly lost, because, in love,
You sent Your Son to save the lost. Amen.

Walk in the Light

This is the message we have heard from
Him and declare to you: God is light;
in Him there is no darkness at all.

1 John 1:5

Many things that happen in the world today are symptoms of a sick society. The average person feels unable to confront the evil around him or her, which can give rise to an attitude of complete despair.

Nothing in our modern world can be as appalling as the crucifixion on Golgotha. And yet the Light broke through that darkest moment in history, when Jesus overcame the forces of evil and rose triumphantly from the dead.

Regardless of how dark your circumstances may be, put your trust in Christ, follow Him and you will see how His light expels the darkness from your life.

Lord Jesus, in Your light we can see light.
Help us to see Your light in this dark world
so that the darkness will be dispersed. Amen.

Take Heart!

Be strong and take heart,
all you who hope in the LORD.

Psalm 31:24

While we are holding on to God's promises, our courage will grow and become strong. God didn't say that we would never be tempted or suffer trials, but He did promise that He will keep us safe.

The most enriching experience is not found in superficial pleasures, but in our most painful sorrow. If we hold on courageously in faith, sorrow serves a holy purpose in our lives.

Romans 8:18 states, "I consider that our present sufferings are not worth comparing with the glory that will be revealed in us." Therefore, take heart!

Loving Father, renew my courage and release me
from my fears. Strengthen me to follow
in the steps of Christ Jesus, my Savior. Amen.

I Will Always
Have Hope

As for me, I will always have hope; I will praise
You more and more. My mouth will tell of Your
righteousness, of Your salvation all day long.

Psalm 71:14-15

What an incredible privilege it is to tell others of the
wonderful things that God has done for you. Recall
God's protection and guidance in your life and tell
someone about how He has helped you in the past.

Place your trust and hope in God. Believe that He
will never leave you but will strengthen you and be
with you in every time of trial and affliction. Let the
psalmist's praises be your example and may you also
have such a passion to declare the praise of God as
long as you live.

Loving Master, I am overwhelmed at all that
You have done and I want to be a witness to
Your goodness to everyone I meet. Amen.

Open the Eyes of My Heart

I pray also that the eyes of your heart may
be enlightened in order that you may know
the hope to which He has called you, the
riches of His glorious inheritance in the saints.

Ephesians 1:18-19

At the time of writing this, Paul was confined to a
prison cell in Rome, under the constant watch of
the Roman guard. But who could possibly tell from
his prayer that anything was wrong! Paul's faithful
description of God's power does not allow even a
hint of hopelessness or despair. Instead he talks of
the "glorious inheritance" of a future in heaven.

Paul's eventual hope was not in earthly people,
but in heaven, eternity and God. The eyes of his heart
could see clearly. Are the eyes of your heart open?

Wonderful Redeemer, help me, through Your
Holy Spirit, to grasp the wonderful future
that You have made possible for me. Amen.

Praise the Lord!

"Praise the Lord and sing praises to Him,
all you peoples." May the God of hope
fill you with all joy and peace as you trust
in Him, so that you may overflow with
hope by the power of the Holy Spirit.

Romans 15:11, 13

We praise and honor the birth of David's descendant, our Lord and Savior, Jesus Christ. We place all our hope in Him for our salvation. Pray daily that you will find hope and peace in Him.

"May the God of hope fill you with all joy and peace as you trust in Him, so that you may overflow with hope by the power of the Holy Spirit." What a blessed way for one person to greet another!

Take time out and thank God for His hope. Allow it to spill over into every aspect of your life.

Lord Jesus, may all people on earth experience
Your hope, peace and joy today. Amen.

Trust in God Alone

In Him our hearts rejoice, for we trust in His holy
name. May Your unfailing love rest upon us,
O LORD, even as we put our hope in You.

Psalm 33:21-22

We all need a sense of security. When difficult situations threaten to overwhelm us, most of us lean heavily on family and friends for help and support. But this prayer reminds us that, in the long run, only the Almighty God can protect and save us.

It is fitting to admit our dependence on the Lord when we come to Him in prayer. Remember that He is our Shield and Protector. As we focus on this wonderful truth, our fear will turn into praise.

Become quiet for a few minutes and think about the ways in which you seek security, in both big and small situations. Then confess to God that, in future, you will trust fully in Him alone.

Lord Jesus, our hope and salvation surround us with
Your unfathomable love and protection. Amen.

The Ways of God

Then my soul will rejoice in the LORD and
delight in His salvation. My whole being
will exclaim, "Who is like You, O LORD?"

Psalm 35:9-10

The splendor of all people fades in comparison with
the mighty deeds of God. One day all people will
bow before God in worship and declare His might
and justice with loud cries. On this day all honor and
glory will be given to Him.

But don't wait for that day. In your prayer time
today, follow David's example and praise and thank
God for saving you and allowing you to put your
trust and hope in Him.

Loving Father, no one can compare with You.
Therefore I will praise You as long as I live. Amen.

Praise for God's Power

The seas have lifted up their voice. Mightier than
the thunder of the great waters, mightier than the
breakers of the sea – the Lord on high is mighty.

Psalm 93:3-4

Through the ages people have marveled at the
wonders of God's creation; especially the seas. The
angry waves that break against the rocks and crash
along the coast demonstrate the overwhelming
power of water.

And yet, as powerful as the water is, the might
of the God who created everything far surpasses
all the powers of nature. Nothing in nature can be
compared to the might of God.

If God's power is so much greater than the might
of nature, He can undoubtedly handle any human
problems. Don't allow desperate situations to undermine your trust in God. Remember that God is
mightier than the waters of the sea.

Creator God, we praise and glorify You because You
are mightier than any created force in nature. Amen.

Divine Protection

They remembered that God was their Rock,
that God most High was their Redeemer.

Psalm 78:35

Many times in the history of the world it seemed as if all was lost and all hope was gone.

Yet God has saved people and nations from devastation in miraculous ways, and has enabled them to overcome dangers and transform defeat into glorious victory.

These cases should serve as a constant reminder of the victorious omnipotence of God in all spheres of life. No circumstances are too small or too big for Him, and no prayer will remain unheard or unanswered. Only in Him will you find deliverance from your distress.

Lord my God, You are a safe fortress to me,
a shield against every calamity that threatens
to overwhelm me. Knowing this, I step
with confidence into the unknown. Amen.

Omnipotent Protector

The LORD is my rock, my fortress and
my deliverer; my God is my rock,
in whom I take refuge.

2 Samuel 22:2-3

When we are afflicted and needy, the love and omnipotence of God protects us. We can overcome any challenge, adversity or problem if we only steadfastly trust in His loving care and grace.

He will command His angels to watch over us and protect us from any danger. We will not be overwhelmed by evil and left powerless. The ability He gives us to choose between what is good and right and what is wrong, will help us to act wisely.

Through the love that is in our hearts, we give and receive love. Then peace and joy fill our minds and hearts, and we are assured that we have an omnipotent Protector.

Father, I bow before You in grateful humility
because You have given me Your light and Your
wisdom so that I can always do what is right. Amen.

The Presence of God

The angel of the LORD encamps around those
who fear Him, and He delivers them.

Psalm 34:7

Faith in the abiding presence of God is strengthened
when you allow Christ to take full control of your life.
To ensure that this truth becomes an inextricable
part of you, it must become an integral part of your
life and mind. If you constantly reaffirm this truth,
not only on bright sunny days but also on dark days,
it will become part of your nature. You will just know
that God is surrounding and enfolding you with His
holy presence.

If you turn to Him purposefully in every dark
moment, He can and will become a constant reality.
If it feels as if He is distant at this moment, then
you need to do something about your relationship
with Him. Reaffirm His living presence in your life by
surrendering and committing yourself to Him anew.

Thank You, my Savior, that I am not controlled
by my emotions but that I can hold on to You. Amen.

The Love of God

I love the LORD, for He heard my
voice; He heard my cry for mercy.

Psalm 116:1

There comes a time in each of our lives when we urgently need reassurance for peace of mind and to calm our spirit.

Regardless of how self-assured you may be, there will come a time in your life when you will recognize that you have such a need. But what if there is no one to assist you in your crucial time? What are you supposed to do then?

The answer lies in today's Scripture verse. God is always there as a refuge and help in time of need. He is always there when you need Him, He always hears when you call to Him from the depths and you can be assured that He will answer your prayers.

O Lord, my God, I love You with all my
heart and know that all things happen
for my good because You love me. Amen.

I Am with You!

"When you pass through the waters, I will be with
you; and when you pass through the rivers,
they will not sweep over you. When you walk
through the fire, you will not be burned;
the flames will not set you ablaze."

Isaiah 43:2

It requires great faith and a strong character to be able to work through adversity and disappointment.

The Lord never promised that our lives would be trouble-free just because we choose to serve Him. But He did promise to be there for us at all times, and help us over life's hurdles. Knowing that you don't have to tackle the afflictions of life on your own is a comforting and reassuring thought.

When problems mar your view, turn to Christ. He is your heavenly Companion. Overcome your problems in the peace of His presence.

Thank You, omnipotent Father, that I can say with
confidence that You are with me day by day. Amen.

A Safe Haven

The Lord is my rock and my fortress and my
deliverer; my God, my strength, in whom I will
trust; my shield and the horn of my salvation.

Psalm 18:2 NKJV

We all seek shelter at one time or another. It may be
in the security of your home, or a shelter against the
wind and rain.

Our spiritual and intellectual faculties are also
often ravaged by the storms of life. We all need a safe
and secure haven where we can find shelter from
these storms and be protected from devastating
emotional consequences.

Even when it seems as if everything is lost, en-
trust yourself to the love of Jesus Christ. However
dark the road ahead may seem, Christ, in His love, is
your shelter and safe haven.

Thank You, my God, that I find
shelter in You and that I will be
safe now and for all eternity. Amen.

God Is a Refuge

Is any one of you in trouble? He should pray.
Is anyone happy? Let him sing songs of praise.

James 5:13

When we face a crisis, prayer is sadly only used as a last desperate act when all other efforts have failed.

Even though we are encouraged to call on God throughout Scripture, the average person looks for human solutions first, rather than considering God's loving invitation.

Over and over He promises His assistance and grace to those who call on Him in their time of need.

Regardless of what the crisis in your life may be, lay your problem before Him in trust and He will transform your crisis into a blessing.

Father, I am experiencing a crisis. Give me Your peace
so that I can see things from Your perspective
and make the right decisions. Amen.

Your Anchor in Life

There is no one holy like the LORD; there is no one besides You; there is no Rock like our God.

1 Samuel 2:2

When faced with problems, some people turn to professional counselors for advice, medical assistance or friends, while others try to fight their way through the dilemma in their own strength.

While all these methods can provide some help, they can't provide assurance that the problem won't occur again, or that the person will be able to handle it if it does. The only sure and lasting solution comes from God.

Never make the mistake of leaving God out of your life. Other things can help you survive, but only God can give you abiding peace.

Savior, by putting my life in Your hands
I know that all things work together for
my benefit because You love me. Amen.

A God Who Encourages

May the God who gives endurance
and encouragement give you a spirit of unity
among yourselves as you follow Christ Jesus.

Romans 15:5

If you reach the point in life where you feel discouraged and unable to cope, it is good to spend quality time in the presence of God. There you will receive the encouragement that only He can give.

Be still and surrender yourself anew to Him, and remember that He is God. In the silence of His divine presence, you can recall all His glorious promises of encouragement. Remember that in both the storm and the stillness, God is with you. He does not want you to remain in the dark valley of despondency; He will give you the strength to complete the task He has set before you.

Holy God, when life is too much for me, I withdraw
into Your presence and there I find the comfort
and the strength that I need. Amen.

Feeling Discouraged?

Say to those with fearful hearts, "Be strong,
do not fear; your God will come."

Isaiah 35:4

We all feel discouraged sometimes. It manifests itself in different ways, but always leaves you feeling disillusioned, wondering whether all your efforts were worth the trouble. Only those who strive for a goal can be discouraged.

Ask God to help you. He wants to see you overcome the effects of discouragement and move forward towards your goal. You do not have to fight alone against discouragement. God is on your side and He is ready to lift you up so that you can continue with joy.

I thank You, heavenly Father, that through
the power of Your Holy Spirit I can triumph
over any discouragement. Amen.

God Keeps His Promises

The LORD is my helper; I will not be afraid.
What can man do to me?

Hebrews 13:6

We have assurance that God will never leave us nor forsake us. God never makes empty promises, and in His omnipotence and grace He keeps His word. He is the God who makes His promises come true even when circumstances seem to prove the opposite.

While Jacob was on the run, he received this promise: "I will watch over you, wherever you go" (Gen. 28:15). How wonderfully God kept that promise! Before David's death, he encouraged his son, Solomon: "Do not be afraid or discouraged, for the Lord God, my God, is with you. He will not fail you" (1 Chron. 28:20). And God did just that!

God is righteous and holy; He is gracious and good and He will never forget you. Whatever He promises, He can and will do!

Loving Father, thank You that I can depend
on Your promises forever. Amen.

God Hears My Cry

I call to the LORD, who is worthy of praise,
and I am saved from my enemies.

2 Samuel 22:4

There is no greater feeling than arriving home safely after a dangerous journey. We like to tell others about our adventures, but we often forget to worship God with prayers of praise for granting us safe passage.

When God delivers us out of desperate situations, we should remember to come quietly before Him for a while and thank Him for what He has done.

How many evils does God protect us from daily? How often have we felt His loving protection over our lives and our loved ones? How can we then forget to thank Him in prayerful worship?

I worship You, Lord my God, because You
have saved me from so much evil. Amen.

From Where Does My Help Come?

I lift up my eyes to the hills – where does my help come
from? My help comes from the LORD, the Maker of
heaven and earth. He will not let your foot slip –
He who watches over you will not slumber.

Psalm 121:1-3

The role of security guards is to protect a building
from intruders. If guards do not pay attention to
their surroundings, then intruders easily slip in.

The Lord never loses concentration while He
watches over you. He watches over you constantly
to make sure that you do not stumble or fall. Our
God never loses focus.

The one who prays knows that God will protect
him because God, who made the heavens and the
earth, who neither slumbers nor sleeps, is able to
protect His children perfectly at all times.

I thank You, Almighty God, that You watch over me day
and night, and keep me safe from all danger. Amen.

Trust in the Lord Forever

The name of the LORD is a strong tower;
the righteous run to it and are safe.

Proverbs 18:10

We all want to feel safe from the attack of enemies and strangers. In this prayer of praise from Isaiah, believers declare that their safety is in the Lord.

In biblical times, in Israel, safety meant being able to live in a city with strong walls that would keep the enemy out. However, walls of stone can collapse, but our God will be able to protect and guard the righteous forever. Therefore believers need never fear anyone!

Allow this Scripture passage to encourage you to focus your thoughts on the Almighty God. Reaffirm your trust in Him today and experience the peace that this kind of trust can bring.

Sovereign God, help me to focus my thoughts
on You and to trust You at all times, because
You are my protector and my eternal Rock. Amen.

Our Hiding Place

The LORD is a refuge for the oppressed, a stronghold
in times of trouble. Those who know Your name
will trust in You, for You, LORD, have
never forsaken those who seek You.

Psalm 9:9-10

David went through intense suffering in his life. He was a fugitive from King Saul, the mightiest man in the land, and on one occasion even his own son turned against him.

Therefore, when David praised God for being a refuge for people in danger, he was not talking in hypothetical or abstract terms. Placing his trust in God was a matter of life or death for him. And God never let him down.

In times of trial and tribulation, remember that God always watches over you. He will never forsake those who call upon Him, nor let them down.

Thank You, mighty God, that we can find a safe refuge
in You and that we can hide in You. Thank You that
You never turn away those who come to You. Amen.

He Watches Over You

O LORD, how many are my foes! How many
rise up against me! Many are saying of me,
"God will not deliver him." But You are
a shield around me. I lie down and sleep;
I wake again, because the LORD sustains me.

Psalm 3:1-3, 5

If enemies are pursuing you and trying to make you
doubt the power of God's deliverance by saying,
"God will not deliver you," then do what David
did – call on God, who is your shield and protection.
If you do this, then you will be able to lie down and
sleep in peace, because God will watch over you.

There is no need to ever be afraid because God is
our protector. He always looks after His children; He
will never stop looking after us.

Lord, my loving God, I know that You watch over me
because You are my shield and protection. Amen.

Let God's Love Guide You

You have made known to me the path of life;
You will fill me with joy in Your presence,
with eternal pleasures at Your right hand.

Psalm 16:11

For many people life has lost its purpose. Day after day they plod through a monotonous cycle. This is totally unnecessary. The future belongs to God ... and to you! When you put God first in your life, He becomes your inspiration and He will lead you every day as He promised.

Be adamant about getting to know God better through regular Bible study and persevering prayer. Then you will discover that past failures really belong to the past while the future is bright and promising. Live with Christ every day and you will experience a new quality of life. You will receive only the best from Him if you allow Him to guide you in His love.

Dear Lord, thank You that I can abide in You.
Thank You for teaching me how to live
and for giving me Your joy. Amen.

God Is My Refuge

Your word is a lamp to my
feet and a light for my path.

Psalm 119:105

In this Scripture verse, the lamp symbolizes the guidance, wisdom and knowledge that we find in the Word.

This life is like a dark wilderness through which we must find a way and, just as a lamp helps a traveler in the dark, the Word is a light on our path so we will not stumble.

Pray for light and truth from God's Word so that you can stay on the path of life. Ask God to guide you through the situations that could become stumbling blocks on your spiritual path and commit yourself anew to Him and His Word today.

Thank You, merciful God, that You light up
our dark path with the light of Your Word.
Help us to use Your light each day. Amen.

Your Only Hope

Revive us, and we will call on Your name.
Restore us, O LORD God Almighty; make Your
face shine upon us, that we may be saved.

Psalm 80:18-19

When you come to the end of your own reserves and find yourself worn out, there is only one place to which you can flee for refuge. God is your only hope for strength.

God created you to fellowship with Him; He wants you to call on His name. You are the branches of His vine and therefore you are completely dependent on the One who planted you – God Himself.

Thank God for the refuge He offers you and for the love that He showers on you. And when you feel that you cannot go on, ask Him once again to renew your strength for the road that you must follow.

Provider God, let Your holy countenance shine down
on us in love and provide our basic needs. Amen.

Stay Close to the Shepherd

Even when I walk through the darkest valley, I will
not be afraid, for you are close beside me. Your
rod and Your staff protect and comfort me.

Psalm 23:4 NLT

Scripture never tries to hide the dark shadows of life.
This Scripture verse describes how God is always
with us, even in the valley of the shadow of death.
Therefore we should fear no evil because God is
always with us.

From time to time we should recall the moments
in our lives where God was with us in the valley.
Stay close to Him because He will always be with us,
through the rest of the year and for the rest of our
lives, because He promised to never leave us.

Omnipresent God, even when I walk through the valley
of the shadow of death, I will not fear, because
I know that You are always close to me. Amen.

Rest in God's Care

Show the wonder of Your great love, You who
save by Your right hand those who take
refuge in You from their foes. Keep me
as the apple of Your eye; hide me
in the shadow of Your wings.

Psalm 17:7-8

You are the apple of the Lord's eye. God will protect you because He will answer your cries of distress; He is bending down, compassionate and interested in your prayer.

Believe in your heart that God will use His power to protect you. When you look to God with expectation, you receive the protection you so desperately seek.

Let this Scripture verse remind you that God is willing and able to protect you. He is the only One who can protect you, so lay your cares at His feet.

I thank You, Almighty God, that You protect
me as the apple of Your eye. Hide me in
the shadow of Your wings. Amen.

Seek Shelter with God

My eyes are fixed on You, O Sovereign LORD; in You
I take refuge – do not give me over to death.
Keep me from the snares they have laid for me.

Psalm 141:8-9

A newspaper carried a report about a hiker who got lost and walked through a blinding snowstorm for hours without any sign of life. Exhausted, hungry and almost frozen to death, he was ready to give up hope when he spotted a cabin between the trees.

How welcoming the sight of that cabin must have seemed to the hiker – his refuge and safe fortress. It literally saved his life.

Jesus Christ represents that cabin for us – He is our refuge against the dangers surrounding us. Therefore it is comforting to know that when enemies surround us, we can call on God to deliver us. Cast all your cares and concerns onto God, He is your refuge and safe fortress.

Savior and Redeemer, today I look to You for help.
Please open Your hand and provide in all my needs. Amen.

Secure in God

In the beginning You laid the foundations of the earth,
and the heavens are the work of Your hands. They
will perish, but You remain; they will all wear out
like a garment. But You remain the same,
and Your years will never end.

Psalm 102:25-27

Are you going through a time of great affliction and misery? Allow the words of this Scripture verse to soothe your worried soul and provide a ray of hope in your desperate situation.

Remember, you are a child of God. This God rises above all our problems, as well as above time and space. He is willing and able to keep His children safe and to let them live in His holy presence forever.

Should you find yourself in distress today because of the problems of life, then let God know of your anxieties and thank Him for providing stability in your ever-changing world.

O God, my refuge and my fortress, thank You for
the security that You bring into my life. Amen.

Take Refuge in God

I will sing of Your strength, in the morning I will
sing of Your love; for You are my fortress, my
refuge in times of trouble. O my Strength,
I sing praise to You; You, O God,
are my fortress, my loving God.

Psalm 59:16-17

Love between people can be a source of great joy or
of great pain – especially if someone's love is fickle
and unpredictable.

However, with God as your Savior, you need never
feel that His love is fickle. In contrast to human love,
God's love is infallible!

Because of this you can count on God to always
be your refuge in times of trouble. When you
experience difficult times, find your power, strength
and refuge in the infallible love of God. It will never
fail you.

Holy God, I seek Your shelter in times of
difficulty and affliction. As I turn to You,
let me experience Your infallible love. Amen.

Turn Anxiety into Joy

In this you greatly rejoice, though now
for a little while you may have had to suffer grief
in all kinds of trials. These have come so
that your faith may be proved genuine.

1 Peter 1:6-7

There are times in life when everything seems empty, dismal and dreary. The good news of the Christian faith is that you are never alone.

However, you must believe that Christ is your Savior and fully trust in Him. Then you have the glorious assurance that you need never struggle with your problems and anxieties alone. He promised to be with you always.

If you do this, you will experience the peace that surpasses all understanding.

How often, O Lord, did You not turn my anxiety into joy! I
will never be able to thank You enough for that! Amen.

When Things Go Wrong

Do not be afraid or discouraged because of this
vast army. For the battle is not yours, but God's.

2 Chronicles 20:15

Sometimes you may feel that there is no reason for
you to continue fighting the battle. You feel defeated and want to give up.

When these feelings get the better of you, you
have probably ignored God. Overwhelmed by the
forces against you, you have allowed the influence
of evil to affect you negatively. By displaying such
an attitude, you have subconsciously acknowledged
that these forces have greater control over your life
than your heavenly Father.

Hold on to the timeless truth, to your loyalty to
God, and to everything He represents. Choose to
join forces with the dynamic power of justice. Then
no destructive force can stand against you.

Lord, help me to count my blessings during crises.
You will never abandon me. Even in difficult
times I can count on Your blessings. Amen.

Our Loving Protector

For the eyes of the LORD range
throughout the earth to strengthen those
whose hearts are fully committed to Him.

2 Chronicles 16:9

Let us never think that we have drifted out of the sphere of God's love. We read in His Word that His eyes range throughout the earth in order to help those who put their trust in Him. The Lord always knows who places their expectations in Him: He shelters them in times of danger, helps them handle temptations and problems, and comforts them in their sorrow.

What a blessed privilege it is to have such a God as our protector. Wherever we find ourselves while living within His will, we can rest assured that His eyes keep a loving watch over us and that He is ready to hear when we call and to help when we need Him.

We praise Your great name, God, because You
never forsake those who trust in You. Amen.

Cheerful in the Face of Adversity

All the days of the oppressed are wretched,
but the cheerful heart has a continual feast.

Proverbs 15:15

One of the most valuable gifts that the Holy Spirit has bestowed upon God's children is the gift of contagious gladness and joy. However, even the Christian's life is subject to tides of ever-changing emotions. The life of our Lord is an excellent example of this as He also experienced the heights and depths of the spirit.

It is impossible for a Christian to always smile. There are times when you would much rather cry. However, when we set our minds on Christ, a peaceful spirit is established and this generates real joy and gladness.

I praise and thank You, Lord my God, that I can live
joyfully and trustingly because Your Spirit dwells in me.

Amen.

God Performs His Wonders through You

Cast all your anxiety on Him because He cares for you.

1 Peter 5:7

Sometimes worries beyond your control prey on your mind; you may be concerned about your job, or an increase in rent. If you are anxious and worried about a personal matter, you must remember that God is greater than all the circumstances and situations that could befall you.

For a moment you may have allowed fear and uncertainty about the future to obscure your image of God. However, He is forever constant and He desires to share the deepest experience of your life with you. God's omnipotence will sweep away all petty thoughts and all uncertainty will disappear.

Your works are perfect, Lord, and even when I drink
from the cup of bitterness; You will never forsake
me but will help me to understand that,
with You, I will survive. Amen.

God Hears Your Cry

I call on the LORD in my distress, and He answers me.

Psalm 120:1

It is essential for you to realize that you are never completely alone and that you are not without friends in this world. Jesus, the living Christ, has promised to never leave nor forsake you.

He offers you His friendship and all that He asks from you is to be obedient to His commandment of love.

Secure in this knowledge, you have the assurance of His constant presence in your life. He has already heard your call of distress and answered your prayer.

You know our deepest sorrow and hear our
sighs. Help us, Lord, never to forget that You
alone are our salvation and support. Amen.